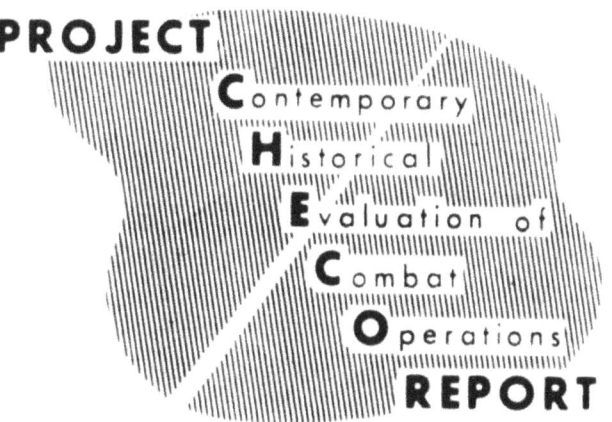

PROJECT CHECO REPORT

Contemporary Historical Evaluation of Combat Operations

Impact of Darkness and Weather on Air Operations in SEA

10 MARCH 1969

HQ PACAF

Directorate, Tactical Evaluation
CHECO Division

Prepared by:

Lt Col Philip R. Harrison

Project CHECO 7th AF, DOAC

PROJECT CHECO REPORTS

The counterinsurgency and unconventional warfare environment of Southeast Asia has resulted in the employment of USAF airpower to meet a multitude of requirements. The varied applications of airpower have involved the full spectrum of USAF aerospace vehicles, support equipment, and manpower. As a result, there has been an accumulation of operational data and experiences that, as a priority, must be collected, documented, and analyzed as to current and future impact upon USAF policies, concepts, and doctrine.

Fortunately, the value of collecting and documenting our SEA experiences was recognized at an early date. In 1962, Hq USAF directed CINCPACAF to establish an activity that would be primarily responsive to Air Staff requirements and direction, and would provide timely and analytical studies of USAF combat operations in SEA.

Project CHECO, an acronym for Contemporary Historical Evaluation of Combat Operations, was established to meet this Air Staff requirement. Managed by Hq PACAF, with elements at Hq 7AF and 7/13AF, Project CHECO provides a scholarly, "on-going" historical evaluation and documentation of USAF policies, concepts, and doctrine in Southeast Asia combat operations. This CHECO report is part of the overall documentation and evaluation which is being accomplished. Along with the other CHECO publications, this is an authentic source for an assessment of the effectiveness of USAF airpower in SEA.

MILTON B. ADAMS, Major General, USAF
Chief of Staff

REPLY TO ATTN OF: DOTEC

10 March 1969

SUBJECT: Project CHECO Report, "Impact of Darkness and Weather on Air Operations in SEA" (U)

TO: SEE DISTRIBUTION PAGE

1. Attached is a SECRET NOFORN document. It shall be transported, stored, safeguarded, and accounted for in accordance with applicable security directives. SPECIAL HANDLING REQUIRED, NOT RELEASABLE TO FOREIGN NATIONALS. The information contained in this document will not be disclosed to foreign nationals or their representatives. Retain or destroy in accordance with AFR 205-1. Do not return.

2. This letter does not contain classified information and may be declassified if attachment is removed from it.

FOR THE COMMANDER IN CHIEF

WARREN H. PETERSON, Colonel, USAF
Chief, CHECO Division
Directorate, Tactical Evaluation
DCS/Operations

1 Atch
Proj CHECO Rprt (SNF),
10 Mar 69

DISTRIBUTION LIST

	NO. OF COPIES			NO. OF COPIES

1. SECRETARY OF THE AIR FORCE

    a. SAFAA 1
    b. SAFLL 1
    c. SAFOI 2

2. HEADQUARTERS USAF

    a. AFBSA 1

    b. AFCCS

        (1) AFCCSSA 1
        (2) AFCVC 1
        (3) AFCAV 1
        (4) AFCVD 1
        (5) AFCHO 2

    c. AFCSA 1

        (1) AFCSAC. 1
        (2) AFCSAM. 1

    d. AFGOA 2

    e. AFIGO

        (1) AFIIN 1
        (2) AFISI 3
        (3) AFISL 1

    f. AFMSG 1

    g. AFNIN

        (1) AFNIE 1
        (2) AFNINA. 1
        (3) AFNINCC 1
        (4) AFNINED 4

    h. AFAAC 1

        (1) AFAMA 1
        (2) AFAMAI. 1

    i. AFODC 1

        (1) AFOAP 1
        (2) AFOAPS. 1
        (3) AFOCC 1
        (4) AFOCE 1
        (5) AFOMO 1
        (6) AFOMOAC 1
        (7) AFOWX 1

    j. AFPDC

        (1) AFPDP 1
        (2) AFPMDG. 1
        (3) AFPDW 1
        (4) AFPMRE. 1

    k. AFRDC 1

        (1) AFRDD 1
        (2) AFRDQ 1
        (3) AFRDR 1
        (4) AFRDF 1

    l. AFSDC 1

        (1) AFSLP 1
        (2) AFSME 1
        (3) AFSMS 1
        (4) AFSPD 1
        (5) AFSSS 1
        (6) AFSTP 1

    m. AFTAC 1

n. AFXDC

    (1) AFXDO 1
    (2) AFXDOC. 1
    (3) AFXDOD. 1
    (4) AFXDOL. 1
    (5) AFXOP 1
    (6) AFXOSL. 1
    (7) AFXOSN. 1
    (8) AFXOSO. 1
    (9) AFXOSS. 1
    (10) AFXOSV. 1
    (11) AFXOTR. 1
    (12) AFXOTW. 1
    (13) AFXOTZ. 1
    (14) AFXPD 6

        (a) AFXPPGS 3

3. MAJOR COMMANDS

  a. TAC

    (1) HEADQUARTERS

        (a) DO. 1
        (b) DPL 2
        (c) DOCC. 1
        (d) DORQ. 1
        (e) DIO 1

    (2) AIR FORCES

        (a) 9AF

            1. DO. 1
            2. DP. 1

        (b) 12AF

            1. DORF. . . . 1
            2. DP. 1
            3. DI. 1

        (c) 19AF

            1. DO. 1
            2. DP. 1
            3. DA-C. . . . 1

        (d) USAFSOF

            1. DO 1
            2. DI 1

    (3) AIR DIVISIONS

        (a) 831AD(DO). 2
        (b) 832AD(DO). 2
        (c) 833AD(DDO) 2
        (d) 835AD(DO). 2
        (e) 836AD(DO). 2
        (f) 838AD

            1. DO 1
            2. DOCP 1

        (g) 839AD(DO). 2
        (h) 840AD. 2

    (4) WINGS

        (a) 1SOW(DO) 1
        (b) 4TFW(DO) 1
        (c) 15TFW(DO). 1
        (d) 23TFW(DOI) 1
        (e) 27TFW(DOP) 1
        (f) 33TFW(DOI) 1
        (g) 49TFW(DCOI). 1
        (h) 64TFW. 1
        (i) 67TRW(C) 1
        (j) 75TRW(DO). 1
        (k) 78FW(WGODC). 1
        (l) 82CSPW(DOCH) 1
        (m) 123TRW 1
        (n) 140TFW(CA) 1
        (o) 313TAW(DOPL) 1
        (p) 316TAW(DOP). 1
        (q) 317TAW(EX) 1
        (r) 363TRW 1
        (s) 464TAW(DO) 1
        (t) 474TFW(TFOX) 1
        (u) 479TFW 1
        (v) 516TAW(DOPL) 1
        (w) 4410CCTW(DOTR) . . . 1
        (x) 4442CCTW(DO) 1
        (y) 4453CCTW(DO) 1
        (z) 4500ABW(DO). 1
       (aa) 4510CCTW(DO16-I) . . 1

    (bb) 4525FWW(FWOA) . . . 1
    (cc) 4531TFW(DOI) 1
    (dd) 4554CCTW(DOI) . . . 1

   (5) TAC CENTERS, SCHOOLS

    (a) USAFTAWC

     <u>1</u>. DA 2

    (b) USAFTARC

     <u>1</u>. DID 2

    (c) USAFTALC

     <u>1</u>. DCRL 2

    (d) USAFTFWC

     <u>1</u>. CRCD 2

    (e) USAFSOC(DO) 2
    (f) USAFAGOS(DAB-C) . . 2

b. SAC

 (1) HEADQUARTERS

  (a) DOPL 1
  (b) DPLF 1
  (c) DM 1
  (d) DI 1

 (2) AIR FORCES

  (a) 2AF(DICS) 1
  (b) 8AF(C) 1
  (c) 15AF 1

 (3) AIR DIVISIONS

  (a) 3AD(DO) 3

c. MAC

 (1) HEADQUARTERS

  (a) MAOID 1
  (b) MAOCO 1
  (c) MAFOI 1
  (d) MACOA 1

 (2) AIR FORCES

  (a) 21AF

   <u>1</u>. ODC 1
   <u>2</u>. OCXI . . . 1

  (b) 22AF

   <u>1</u>. ODC 1
   <u>2</u>. OCXI . . . 1

 (3) AIR DIVISIONS

  (a) 322AD 1

 (4) WINGS

  (a) 375AAWG

   <u>1</u>. ODC 1

  (b) 89MAWG

   <u>1</u>. ODC 1

  (c) 60MAWG

   <u>1</u>. ODC 1
   <u>2</u>. OXI 1

  (d) 61MAWG

   <u>1</u>. ODC 1
   <u>2</u>. OIN 1

(e) 62MAWG

    <u>1</u>. OCXP 1
    <u>2</u>. OOPT 1

(f) 63MAWG

    <u>1</u>. O. 1
    <u>2</u>. OCXCI. 1

(g) 435MAWG

    <u>1</u>. ODC. 1
    <u>2</u>. OTI. 1

(h) 436MAWG

    <u>1</u>. O. 1
    <u>2</u>. OCXC 1

(i) 437MAWG

    <u>1</u>. ODC. 1
    <u>2</u>. OCXI 1

(j) 438MAWG

    <u>1</u>. ODC. 1
    <u>2</u>. OCXC 1

(k) 445MAWG

    <u>1</u>. OC. 1
    <u>2</u>. WDO-PLI . . . 1

(5) MAC SERVICES

  (a) AWS

    <u>1</u>. AWXW. 1
    <u>2</u>. AFCSPI. . . . 1

  (b) ARRS

    <u>1</u>. ARXLR 1

  (c) ACGS

    <u>1</u>. AGOV. 1

  (d) AAVS

    <u>1</u>. AVODOD 1

d. ADC

(1) HEADQUARTERS

  (a) ADODC. 1
  (b) ADOOP. 1
  (c) ADOTT. 1
  (d) ADLCC. 1

(2) AIR FORCES

  (a) 1AF

    <u>1</u>. DO 1
    <u>2</u>. DP 1

  (b) 4AF

    <u>1</u>. DO 1
    <u>2</u>. DP 1

  (c) 10AF

    <u>1</u>. DO 1
    <u>2</u>. PDP-P. 1

  (d) 14Aerosp Force

    <u>1</u>. 14ODC-I. . . . 2

  (e) AF Iceland 2

(3) AIR DIVISIONS

  (a) 25AD 2
  (b) 26AD(OIN). 2
  (c) 27AD 2
  (d) 28AD(OIN). 2
  (e) 29AD(ODC). 2
  (f) 31AD 2
  (g) 32AD(ODC-A). . . . 2
  (h) 33AD(OIN). 2
  (i) 34AD(OIN). 2
  (j) 35AD(CCR). 2
  (k) 36AD(OIN). 2
  (l) 37AD(ODC). 2

e. ATC

    (1) HEADQUARTERS

        (a) ATXDC 1

f. AFLC

    (1) HEADQUARTERS

        (a) MCFH 1
        (b) MCGH 1
        (c) MCOO 1

g. AFSC

    (1) HEADQUARTERS

        (a) SCLAP 2
        (b) SCS-6 1
        (c) SCTPL 1
        (d) SCEH 2
        (e) ASD/ASJT . . . 2
        (f) ESD/ESWV . . . 2
        (g) ADTC/ADP . . . 2
        (h) RADC/EMOEL . . 2

h. AFCS

    (1) HEADQUARTERS

        (a) CSOCH 5

i. USAFSS

    (1) HEADQUARTERS

        (a) ODC 1
        (b) CHO 5

    (2) SUBORDINATE UNITS

        (a) Eur Scty Rgn

            1. OPD-P . . . 1

        (b) 6940 Scty Wg

            1. OOD 1

j. AAC

    (1) HEADQUARTERS

        (a) ALDOC-A 2

k. USAFSO

    (1) COH 1
    (2) OOP 1

l. PACAF

    (1) HEADQUARTERS

        (a) DP 1
        (b) DI 1
        (c) DO 1
        (d) DPL 4
        (e) CSH 1
        (f) DOTEC 6
        (g) DE 1
        (h) DM 1

    (2) AIR FORCES

        (a) 5AF

            1. DOPP 1
            2. DP 1

        (b) 7AF

            1. DO 1
            2. DIXA 1
            3. DPL 1
            4. TACC 1
            5. DOAC 2

        (c) 13AF

            1. DOO 1
            2. DXIH 1
            3. DPL 1

        (d) 7AF/13AF

            1. CHECO . . . 3

(3) AIR DIVISIONS

    (a) 313AD(DOP) . . . 2
    (b) 314AD(DOP) . . . 2
    (c) 327AD. 2
    (d) 834AD. 2

(4) WINGS

    (a) 3TFW(DCOP) . . . 1
    (b) 8TFW(DCOA) . . . 1
    (c) 12TFW(DCOI). . . 1
    (d) 14SOW(DCO) . . . 1
    (e) 31TFW(DCOA). . . 1
    (f) 35TFW. 1
    (g) 37TFW(DCOI) . . . 1
    (h) 56SOW. 1
    (i) 315SOW(DCOI) . . 1
    (j) 347TFW(DCOOT). . 1
    (k) 355TFW(DCOC) . . 1
    (l) 366TFW 1
    (m) 388TFW(DCO). . . 1
    (n) 405FW(DCOA). . . 1
    (o) 432TRW(DCOI) . . 1
    (p) 460TRW(DCOI) . . 1
    (q) 475TFW(DCO). . . 1
    (r) 483TAW(DCO). . . 1
    (s) 553RW(DCOI). . . 1
    (t) 633SOW 1
    (u) 6400 Test Sq . . 1

(5) OTHER UNITS

    (a) Task Force ALPHA

        1. DXI. 1

    (b) 504TASG(CA). . . 1

i. USAFE

(1) HEADQUARTERS

    (a) ODC/OA 1
    (b) ODC/OTA. 1
    (c) OOT. 1
    (d) XDC. 1

(2) AIR FORCES

    (a) 3AF(ODC) 2
    (b) 16AF 2

    (c) 17AF

        1. ODC 1
        2. OID 1

(3) WINGS

    (a) 10TRW(OIN/5OA). . . . 1
    (b) 20TFW(CACC) 1
    (c) 26TRW(C). 1
    (d) 36TFW(CADS) 1
    (e) 48TFW(DCOTS). 1
    (f) 50TFW(CACC) 1
    (g) 66TRW(DCOIN-T). . . . 1
    (h) 81TFW 1
    (i) 401TFW(DCOI). 1
    (j) 513TAW(OID) 1
    (k) 601TCW. 1
    (l) 7101ABW(DCO-CP) . . . 1
    (m) 7149TFW(DCOI) 1
    (n) 7272FTW(CAAC) 1

4. SEPARATE OPERATING AGENCIES

a. AFAFC (SAA-12). 1
b. AFDSDC (HCAA) 2
c. ACIC

    (1) ACOMC 2

d. ARPC (RPCAS-22) 2
e. AFRES

    (1) AFROP 2

f. USAFA

    (1) CA. 2
    (2) CMT 1
    (3) DFH 1

g. AU

    (1) AUL(SE)-69-108. 2
    (2) ASI (ASHAF-A) 2
    (3) ASI (ASD-1) 1
    (4) ACSC-SA 1

5. MILITARY DEPARTMENTS, UNIFIED AND SPECIFIED COMMANDS, AND JOINT STAFFS

    a. CINCAL 1
    b. CINCLANT 1
    c. USAFLANT 1
    d. CHIEF, NAVAL OPERATIONS 1
    e. COMMANDANT, MARINE CORPS 1
    f. CINCONAD 1
    g. DEPARTMENT OF THE ARMY 1
    h. JOINT CHIEFS OF STAFF 1
    i. JSTPS 1
    j. CINCPAC 1
    k. SECRETARY OF DEFENSE 1
    l. CINCAFSTRIKE 1
    m. USCINCMEAFSA 1
    n. USCINCEUR 1
    o. COMUSFORAZ 1
    p. COMUSJAPAN 1
    q. COMUSKOREA 1
    r. COMUSMACTHAI 1
    s. COMUSMACV 1
    t. USCINCSO 1
    u. COMUSTDC 1
    v. CINCSTRIKE 1

6. SCHOOLS

    a. Senior USAF Rep, National War College 1
    b. Senior USAF Rep, Industrial College of the Armed Forces 1
    c. Senior USAF Rep, Armed Forces Staff College 1
    d. Senior USAF Rep, US Naval War College 1
    e. Senior USAF Rep, Naval Amphibious School 1
    f. Senior USAF Rep, Marine Corps Education Center 1
    g. Senior USAF Rep, US Army War College 1
    h. Senior USAF Rep, US Army C&G Staff College 1
    i. Senior USAF Rep, US Army Infantry School 1
    j. Senior USAF Rep, US Army JFG Ctr for Special Warfare 1

TABLE OF CONTENTS

	Page
FOREWORD	xiv
INTRODUCTION	xv
CHAPTER I - GEOGRAPHICAL AND METEOROLOGICAL SUMMARY OF SEA	1
Introduction	1
Geographical Features	1
Republic of Vietnam	1
North Vietnam	2
Laos	2
Cambodia	3
Thailand	4
Climatology of Southeast Asia	5
Introduction	5
Northern Mountains Region	5
Chao Phraya Lowlands Region	7
Southwestern Mountains Region	7
Southern Lowlands Region	8
Korat Plateau Region	9
Eastern Highlands Region	9
Eastern Coast Region	10
Southeastern Coast Region	11
Summary	11
CHAPTER II - IMPACT OF DARKNESS AND WEATHER EN ROUTE TO TARGET AREA	13
Problems and Limitations Attributable to Darkness	13
Summary	26
Problems and Limitations Attributable to Weather	27
Summary	35
CHAPTER III - IMPACT OF DARKNESS AND WEATHER ON TARGET ACQUISITION PROCESS	37
Problems and Limitations Attributable to Darkness	37
Summary	52
Problems and Limitations Attributable to Weather	52
Summary	60

		Page
CHAPTER IV	- IMPACT OF DARKNESS AND WEATHER ON TARGET ATTACKS	61
	Problems and Limitations Attributable to Weather	73
	Visual Attacks	73
	Summary	79
	COMBAT SKYSPOT (MSQ-77)	79
	Summary	85
CHAPTER V	- IMPACT OF DARKNESS AND WEATHER ON EGRESS AND RECOVERY	86
	Recovery and Landing	87
	Summary	90
CHAPTER VI	- IMPACT OF DARKNESS AND WEATHER ON AC-47 GUNSHIP OPERATIONS	92
	Background	92
	Problems and Limitations Attributed to Darkness	94
	Conclusions	97
	Lessons Learned	98
CHAPTER VII	- IMPACT OF DARKNESS AND WEATHER ON AIRLIFT AND DEFOLIATION OPERATIONS	100
	Airlift, Airland Operations	100
	Airdrop and Extraction Operations	105
	Airlift Combat Operations	106
	Equipment Requirements	109
	Defoliation Operations	114
	Conclusions	114
	Lessons Learned	116
CHAPTER VIII	- CONCLUSIONS	118

FOOTNOTES

Introduction	122
Chapter I	122
Chapter II	123
Chapter III	126
Chapter IV	128
Chapter V	131
Chapter VI	131
Chapter VII	133

APPENDIXES

    I.   Extracts, 7AF Night Combat Operations Conference 134
   II. Classification of Airfields 140

GLOSSARY 141

FIGURES   <u>Follows Page</u>

    1.   Regional Areas of Southeast Asia 2
    2.   Out-Country Interdiction Areas 20
    3.   Out-Country Operations, Route Packages 42
    4.   Alpha Strike Force Team 54
    5.   Corps Areas 58
    6.   M-117 Guided Bomb, Functional Diagram 78
    7.   COMBAT SKYSPOT Tactical Aircraft Statistics 80
    8.   Total In and Out-Country Sorties (Percentages) 82

FOREWORD

Combine adverse effects of darkness and weather conditions on air operations in a combat situation, and a very hazardous operational environment is likely to prevail. This CHECO report investigates problems and limitations of the impact which darkness and weather have on air operations in Southeast Asia. Throughout this report, special emphasis is placed on tactics, techniques, and innovations developed to counteract unfavorable effects of night and weather on mission accomplishment.

INTRODUCTION

To improve the operational capability of the U.S. Air Force in Southeast Asia, every attempt was made to perfect tactics and techniques which would attain the maximum navigation capability, electronic protection, and bombing accuracy with the possessed equipment.[1] There was an urgent requirement, clearly recognized by Seventh Air Force, for a more effective ordnance delivery capability. At the top of its Master Priority List of more than 100 Active Southeast Asia Operational Requirements (SEAORs), was SEAOR-077, which called for an improved all-weather delivery system. Other high priority SEAORs identified requirements for improving the night/weather reconnaissance capability, target marking and illumination flares, and night attack capability.[2] Several other measures were taken by 7AF in an attempt to improve the effectiveness of its existing night/weather capability. For example, a Night Combat Operations Conference was held on 9-10 September 1968, in Bangkok, Thailand to discuss the various aspects of out-country, night combat operations. Key representatives from all agencies directly involved in these night operations were in attendance. Objectives of this conference were: (1) to cultivate a better understanding of the operating concepts, problems, and peculiarities of the participating units concerned; (2) discuss tactics and techniques and exchange ideas for accomplishing the night operations program with a view toward improving it; and (3) make recommendations concerning night operations, obtain higher authority approval, and promulgate these recommendations in the form of positive action.[3] As a result of this Bangkok Conference, several important recommendations for improving the effectiveness of night operations in SEA were formulated (Appendix I).

Since the primary purpose of this report is to investigate the problems and limitations attributed to night/weather conditions and to describe their impact on air operations in SEA, a typical mission profile is used to place them in proper prospective. For the purpose of this report, the mission profile is divided into these segments:

- En route to target area.
- Target acquisition.
- Target attack.
- Egress from target area.
- Recovery at a designated airfield.

With the exception of the Gunship, Airlift, and Defoliation missions, the impact of night/weather on air operations was related to the different segments of this mission profile.

CHAPTER I

GEOGRAPHICAL AND METEOROLOGICAL SUMMARY OF SOUTHEAST ASIA

Introduction

The role of the United States Air Force in the war in Southeast Asia (Republic of Vietnam, North Vietnam, Laos, Cambodia, and Thailand) covers the entire spectrum of combat operations. These operations are conducted within several, different geographical regions and are flown during conditions of daylight, darkness, and weather. A brief look at the geographical and climatic aspects of these regional areas (Figure 1) is necessary to establish a feel for the night and weather operational environment of Southeast Asia (SEA).

Geographical Features

Republic of Vietnam

Except for a narrow coastal plain and the Mekong River Delta, the Republic of Vietnam is mountainous. The Annam Mountain Range, a series of eroded plateaus extending southward along the Laotian border, is the major geographic feature of Vietnam. Much of that terrain is above 3,000 feet and has higher peaks which range from 6,000 to 8,500 feet. One peak, Ngoc Linh, located 60 miles west of Quang Ngai, rises to a height of 8,524 feet.

Rivers that drain toward the East Coast are short and flow in steep-sided valleys. North of Saigon, the coastal plain is comprised of alluvial terraces and flats, sand dunes, marshlands, and shallow lagoons. In places, this area is broken by spurs of the Annam Range which reach to the sea. The Mekong River flows southward and fans out in the southern portion of the country to form an extensive delta with low-lying swamps and marshlands.[1]

North Vietnam

With the exception of the Red River Delta, which extends inland for about 75 miles, lowlands in North Vietnam are confined to a coastal strip 25 to 40 miles wide. The western and northern portions of the country are mountainous. The ranges are oriented northwest to southeast and, except for small areas in the northwest, are under 5,000 feet in elevation. The highest peak, Fan Si Pan, is located 15 miles southwest of Lao Kay and rises to 10,312 feet. The steep eastern slopes of the Annam Range lie along the Laotian border.[2]

Rivers in North Vietnam flow parallel to mountain ranges, often in deep, narrow gorges, and drain into the Gulf of Tonkin. The coastal plain is composed of alluvial terraces and flats, sand dunes, and shallow lagoons. The southern portion of the plain is broken in places where the spurs of Annam Range reach into the sea.[3]

Laos

The northern half of Laos is comprised of mountains and high

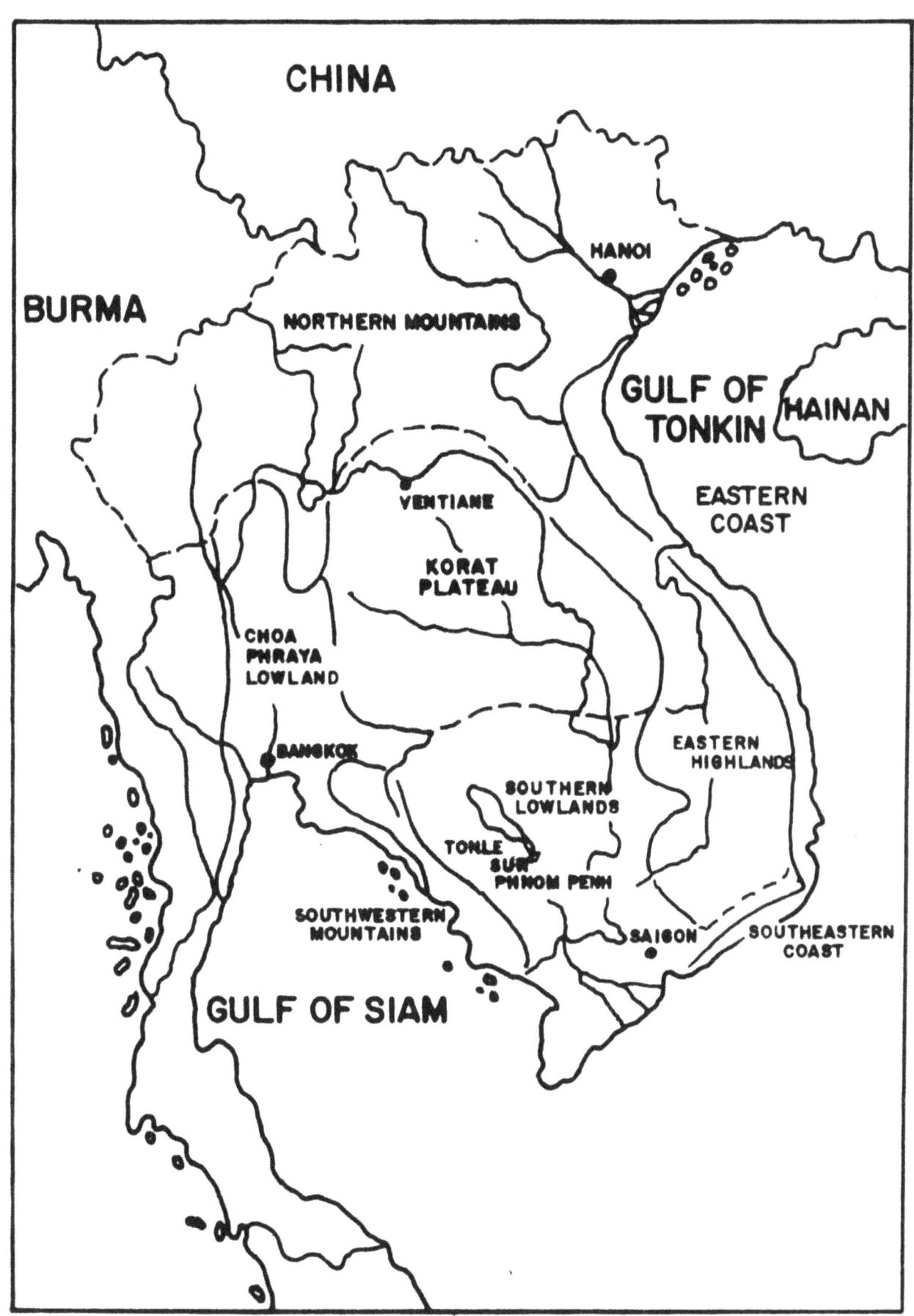

REGIONAL AREAS OF SOUTHEAST ASIA

FIGURE 1

plateau regions cut by deep river valleys. In general, mountain ranges are oriented northeast to southwest. Many peaks extend above 7,000 feet and Phu Bai, located 60 miles northeast of Vientiane, is 9,242 feet high. The southern half of Laos is composed of the Annam Range, along the borders of North Vietnam, Republic of Vietnam, and the alluvial plains, which slope westward to the low-lying valley floor of the Mekong River and Plateau des Bolovens. A number of deep passes, including the two major passes, Deo Keo Nau and Deo Mu Gia, penetrate the Annam Range along the North Vietnam border.

Cambodia

Cambodia has three major geographical features: (1) the Mekong River, which flows through the eastern half of the country; (2) the Tonle Sap, which is a large, shallow lake surrounded by an alluvial plain in the western half of the country; and (3) mountainous regions which are comprised of two major ranges, Chaine de L'Elephant and Chaine des Cardomones, in the Southwest. There are numerous small lakes and marshes east of the Mekong where, except for spurs of the Annam Range in the Republic of Vietnam border region, elevations are generally below 1,000 feet. West of the Mekong River, terrain is almost level. Southwest of the Tonle Sap, beyond the plain, a low broken plateau is backed by high plateaus and mountains with peaks between 3,000 and 5,000 feet in elevation and one peak above 6,000 feet. Several relatively long rivers flow across the alluvial plain and drain into the Tonle Sap. In the Southwest, rivers are short, flow through deep valleys, and drain into the Gulf of Siam after crossing a narrow coastal plain.[4/]

Thailand

Upper Thailand (excluding Peninsular Thailand) has four important geographical features: (1) northern mountains; (2) lowlands; (3) Korat Plateau; and (4) western mountains. The northern mountain region is composed of hills and mountains that are cut by narrow and broad valleys. Except for the Tanen Taunggyi, along the northern border of Burma, these ranges are oriented north and south. Much of this region is above 3,000 feet in elevation with a few, small areas above 5,000 feet. The highest peak, Doi Angka, which is located 35 miles west-southwest of Chiang Mai, rises to 8,468 feet. Extensive lowlands, with elevations generally below 300 feet, cover most of central Thailand and extend northward about 350 miles from the Gulf of Siam. These lowlands are drained by several rivers that merge north of Takhli and fan out south of Takhli as the Chao Phraya. East of the mountain range that bisects upper Thailand lies the Korat Plateau, a broad flat area with elevations mostly below 650 feet. The Korat Plateau is drained by a river system which flows southeastward into the Mekong River, along the Laos border. The western range that extends along the border of Burma, is 350 miles long and about 50 miles wide. The terrain in the northern portion of Thailand is more rugged than that of the southern portion. Much of the terrain in the north is above 3,000 feet with several peaks more than 5,000 feet high.

Peninsular Thailand is studded with mountains, but the major portion of the peninsula is a series of plains and ridges between 400 and 2,000 feet in elevation. There are some peaks between 4,000 and 5,000 feet and one peak, 150 miles north of Song Khla, rises to about 5,900 feet.

Climatology of Southeast Asia

Introduction

The climate of SEA is monsoonal in nature and characterized by two major weather regimes; the southwest monsoon, with predominantly southwesterly, low-level air streams which flow approximately from mid-May to mid-September in the north, and early October in the south; and the northeast monsoon, with northeasterly air streams, from about mid-October in the north and early November to mid-March in the south. Relatively short transitional periods separate these major regimes. Special phenomena form a part of the weather patterns in SEA. These include: fronts, the intertropical convergence zone, typhoons, crachin (prolonged periods of widespread stratus, fog and drizzle, or light rain), land and sea breezes, wind of Laos, upper-level haze, and tornadoes. Rather than discuss these phenomena in detail, only their effects on flying weather in the regional areas of SEA will be considered.[6/]

Northern Mountains Region

Except for crachin conditions over the Red River Delta and adjacent valleys, cloudiness is at a minimum over the Northern Mountains Region during the northeast monsoon. Generally, nights are clear of low clouds, but often there is scattered-to-broken thin cirrus near 30,000 feet.

Scattered cumulus clouds, with bases 2,000 to 3,000 feet usually appear during morning hours with tops near 8,000 feet. Overcasts are rare in mountainous regions, except in the deeper valleys where early morning fogs or strati form but burn off by about 0900 hours, unless reinforced in the east by crachin conditions. Smoke and haze from grass fires sometimes reduce surface and air-to-air visibility and hinder air operations. Over the Red River Delta and adjacent mountain slopes, morning strati, overcast ceilings, are generally about 1,000 to 3,000 feet and about 3,000 to 4,000 feet thick. Solar heating usually causes the stratus decks to break up by late morning, but afternoon cumulus ceilings are frequent. It is not uncommon for overcasts associated with these crachin conditions to persist for several days. 7/

During the southwest monsoon, there is little diurnal change in total cloudiness. Scattered cumulus, broken altocumulus, and cirrus clouds may be expected throughout the night. During the afternoon, broken cumulus and cumulonimbus (tops to 50,000 feet) occur, with ceilings at 1,000 to 3,000 feet and below 1,000 feet in thundershowers. Periods of afternoon overcasts are frequent. In the east, to the leeward side of the mountains, morning stratus ceilings at 1,000 to 2,000 feet are frequent and broken afternoon cumulus with ceilings of 2,000 to 3,000 feet occurs occasionally. Valley fogs are less persistent and, along with smoke and haze, are less frequent than during the northeast monsoon. 8/

Chao Phraya Lowlands Region

The northeast monsoon is the least cloudy period of the year. Scattered to broken cirrus near 30,000 feet is common at night. Scattered cumulus with bases 2,000 to 4,000 feet forms in the morning hours and in the afternoon; occasionally broken ceilings at 1,000 to 3,000 feet may be expected, particularly over the east-facing slopes. Overcasts are rare and early morning fogs or strati, with ceilings below 1,000 feet are frequent, but they usually burn off by about 0900 hours.[9]

There is little diurnal change in total cloudiness during the southwest monsoon. Some scattered cumulus and broken altocumulus and cirrus and cumulonimbus and ceilings at 1,000 to 3,000 feet are common. Visibility is generally good during this season, but early morning fogs may be expected occasionally.[10]

Southwestern Mountains Region

In this region, the northeast monsoon season is less cloudy than the southwest monsoon season. Nights are occasionally free of low clouds but thin broken cirrus may be expected at 30,000 feet. Scattered cumulus with bases at 2,000 to 3,000 feet usually forms in the morning hours, and frequently increases to broken cumulus with tops near 8,000 feet during the afternoon. Valley fogs are frequent during the early morning hours, but usually burn off by 0900 hours.

In the southwest monsoon, cloud masses pile up on the west-facing slopes during the day. Scattered stratocumulus and broken altocumulus and cirrus are common at night. Broken to overcast cumulus and cumulonimbus, (tops to 50,000 feet) with ceilings of 1,000 to 2,000 feet, are common in the afternoon and early evening. Except in showers, visibility is generally good.[11]

Southern Lowlands Region

In the Southern Lowlands, the northeast monsoon is the least cloudy season of the year. Nights are often clear of low clouds but broken cirrus at 30,000 feet is common. Broken to overcast strati, with bases at 1,000 feet or less, frequently form over the major river systems during the early morning hours but burn off around 0900 hours. Scattered cumuli with bases at 2,000 to 3,000 feet and tops at 8,000 feet, often form after 1000 hours and occasionally produce broken ceilings by early afternoon, but overcasts are rare. Visibility is reduced in fog and smoke over the major river systems, and smoke and haze from numerous grass fires reduce visibility in the northern section.

During the southwest monsoon, scattered stratocumulus and broken altocumulus and cirrus are common at night. Broken to overcast cumulus and cumulonimbus, with 2,000 to 4,000 feet ceilings, occur frequently in the afternoon. In heavy thunderstorms, ceilings below 1,000 feet may be expected. Occasionally, broken to overcast early morning strati with ceilings of 1,000 feet or less occur over the major river systems, but these conditions rarely last beyond 0800 hours.[12]

Korat Plateau Region

Cloudiness is at a minimum during the northeast monsoon season. High broken cirri may be expected at night but rarely any low clouds. Scattered cumulus with bases 2,000 to 3,000 feet and tops near 8,000 feet form during the morning hours, but broken cloud conditions in the afternoon are not common. Early morning fogs, which burn off by 0900 hours, and smoke and haze are major restrictions to visibility.[13]

During the southwest monsoon, scattered stratocumulus and broken altocumulus and cirri are common at night. Scattered cumulus form in the morning, and broken cumulus and cumulonimbus, with ceilings at 1,000 to 3,000 feet are common in the afternoon. Early morning fogs occur occasionally, and smoke and haze are less frequent during the northeast monsoon.[14]

Eastern Highlands Region

Cloudiness is generally at a minimum during the northeast monsoon. Valley fogs and clouds, associated with northeasterly airstreams, block northern passes. Nights are occasionally free of low clouds, particularly in the south, but high broken cirri are common. Western slopes are less cloudy than eastern slopes. Scattered cumuli form during the morning hours and frequently become broken with ceilings at 2,000 to 3,000 feet and tops near 8,000 to 10,000 feet on the east-facing slopes during the late afternoon. Early morning fogs in valleys are frequent, but unless reinforced by crachin conditions, particularly in the north, these fogs rarely persist beyond 0900 hours. Smoke and haze are also restrictions to visibility.[15]

During the southwest monsoon, daytime cloudiness piles up on the west-facing slopes, particularly in the south where clouds frequently obscure mountain tops from early to late morning hours. Scattered to broken cumuli, with bases at 2,000 to 3,000 feet, may be expected by late morning hours and broken to overcast cumulus and cumulonimbus are frequent in the afternoon. Ceilings under 1,000 feet are rare, except in early morning up-slope strati, during thunderstorms, and on high mountain peaks.[16]

Eastern Coast Region

The northeast monsoon season is the cloudiest period of the year over this region. Along with broken cirrus clouds near 30,000 feet, overcasts due to early morning coastal stratus clouds are frequent. Ceilings below 1,500 feet (occasionally below 500 feet) and tops near 4,000 to 8,000 feet are characteristic. Although the stratus clouds usually break up by 0900 or 1000 hours and become scattered to occasionally broken afternoon cumulus clouds, they are likely to persist for several consecutive days, particularly in the north. During these conditions, visibilities are usually less than three miles.[17]

During the southwest monsoon, cloudiness is at a relative minimum. Skies are occasionally free of nocturnal low clouds, but broken alto-cumulus and cirri are usually expected. Because of the region's sheltered location, afternoon clouds are usually scattered cumuli with bases at 1,000 to 3,000 feet. The higher bases with the least cloudiness are generally in the south. Thunderstorms occur less frequently than over adjacent regions; they are most likely to happen late in the afternoon or evening. In general, visibility is good (greater than six miles) during this season, particularly in the south.[18/]

Southeastern Coast Region

This region, because of its relative protection from both monsoon seasons, enjoys some of the best all-year flying weather in SEA. During the northeast monsoon cloudiness is similar to that of the Eastern Coast Region, except that cloudiness over east-facing slopes is more abundant and similar to that of the Eastern Highlands Region. During the southwest monsoon, cloudiness is similar to that in the Southern Lowlands Region, except that cloudiness is more abundant over exposed western slopes than along the coast. Fogs are infrequent during the northeast monsoon and rarely occur during the southwest monsoon.[19/]

Summary

The Southeast Asian area is made up of five countries: Republic of Vietnam; North Vietnam; Laos; Cambodia; and Thailand. Within this area are eight geographical regions:

Northern Mountains	Korat Plateau
Chao Phraya Lowlands	Eastern Highlands
Southwestern Mountains	Eastern Coast
Southern Lowlands	Southeastern Coast

The weather in each of these regions is instrumental in making up the total weather picture in SEA. This weather, monsoonal in nature, is characterized by two major regimes: (1) the southwest monsoon with predominantly southwesterly, low-level airstreams flowing roughly from mid-May to September in the north and early October in the south; and (2) the northeast monsoon, with northeasterly airstreams, which flows from approximately mid-October in the north and early November to mid-March in the south. The impact of these weather variations on air operations in SEA will be a vital part of each chapter which follows.

CHAPTER II

IMPACT OF DARKNESS AND WEATHER EN ROUTE TO TARGET AREA

The en route portion of the mission profile includes the takeoff, formation join-up (if applicable), and the ensuing flight to the immediate target area. During this segment of the mission, some of the problems and limitations due to darkness/weather were found to be common to all units: encountered occasionally by some; unique to a few. Throughout this chapter, emphasis is directed toward relating the different aspects of these problems/limitations to the various operational units and aircraft that were assigned to Southeast Asia.

Problems and Limitations Attributable to Darkness

The majority of take offs in SEA were made at high gross weight, and many approached the maximum. Often, replacement pilots had very little experience in heavyweight takeoffs prior to their arrival in SEA. They gained that experience rapidly, but under somewhat other than ideal conditions (namely, in an aircraft fully-loaded with live combat ordnance).[1] Heavily loaded aircraft made formation join-up at night to be one of the most difficult maneuvers performed during the en route phase. Spatial disorientation, difficulty in judging closure and turn rates, and lack of outside references were some of the reasons the 31st TFW developed a standard join-up procedure. The procedure called for all F-100 pilots to accomplish join-up under radar control, above 5,000 feet, at set airspeeds, with the lead aircraft flying straight ahead.[2]

Flight join-up became more complicated as the number of aircraft in the flight increased. Darkness definitely limited the size of a flight that could safely and effectively perform a night, armed reconnaissance or strike mission. After three years of experience, the 8th TFW, employing F-4D aircraft, was convinced that the two-ship flight had proved without exception, the most effective for night operations.[3/] This preference for two-ship formations was found to be common among units flying strike missions.

Maintaining flight integrity during night operations was considered to be a problem by the 366th TFW. This problem was primarily due to the exterior lighting system of F-4s, which provided an unsatisfactory reference for aircraft flying in close, or en route formation. In a join-up from the six o'clock position, the lights provided almost no visual reference for the wingman, until he was extremely close to the lead aircraft. This poor reference was due to the small size and low intensity of the formation lights located on the trailing tips of the wing. When operating over hostile territory, the lead aircraft usually selected a dim, steady light position with the lower fuselage lights turned out. If the wingman's spacing exceeded two-to-four-ship widths under these lighting conditions, sight of the lead aircraft was easily lost. To improve this exterior lighting, the 366th TFW recommended mounting larger lights of higher intensity on the trailing edge of the wing tip, and shielding them on the under side to minimize detection from the ground.[4/]

Inadequate aircraft lighting systems were also experienced by the pilots of the 37th TFW. Join-ups and formation flying caused vertigo and pilot fatigue, due to inadequate exterior lights on their camouflaged F-100s.[5] Aircraft illumination on the F-100 was also considered to be unsatisfactory by the 35th TFW. This deficiency made night join-ups and formation flying more difficult. A solution recommended by the 35th TFW was to expedite completion of T.O. 1F-100-956 (Variable Intensity Light Control) and T.O. 1F-100-1010 (Exterior Flood Lights).[6]

Inadequate interior lighting and location of armament switches were flight safety problems encountered not only by the 35th TFW, but several other units as well. Typical effects of these problems were canopy glare, poor instrument and armament panel lighting, and diversion of the pilot's attention when positioning armament switches. Problems of this type had a serious impact on the pilot's continuous battle against spatial disorientation and vertigo.[7]

The poor reflective characteristics of the camouflage paint on F-105 fighter-bombers flown by the 355th TFW made it difficult for pilots to clearly distinguish the lead aircraft, while flying four-ship formations during certain portions of a mission. This caused eye strain and pilot fatigue. As a remedy to this situation, the Wing requested that night missions be limited to two-ship flights. Radar trail formation was seldom used because aircrews lacked proficiency in this technique. Further, the F-105 radar could not be dimmed sufficiently to prevent a serious loss

15

in the crew's night vision.[8]

The impact of darkness on the operations of units having multiple missions varied for each particular mission. The 388th TFW had three distinct missions; each was performed by specialized aircraft. These missions included: (1) Combat Strike, using F-105D/F and F-4E aircraft; (2) SAM suppression (IRON HAND Operations), using F-105F aircraft, some of which were configured with the "Yokota Modification" to enhance the radar bombing capability; and (3) Night and all-weather strike (COMMANDO NAIL Operations), using F-105F aircraft with the 2098 modification (improved radar presentation and scope photography), EF-105F aircraft with the "Yokota Modification", and F-4E aircraft. Combat strike operations by F-105D/F and F-4E aircraft were flown mostly during daylight hours. Night missions were flown under COMBAT SKYSPOT (ground radar control bombing) control or with the aid of flare light.[9] (These methods are discussed later in the "attack phase" of the mission profile.)

IRON HAND operations included Alpha Strike Force Support with one or two flights of two or four ECM aircraft (Wild Weasel) accompanying 20 or 24 fighter-bomber strike forces into high threat SAM areas; ARC LIGHT (B-52 Strikes) support with single or dual Wild Weasel aircraft in firing position of known SAM sites located in the vicinity of ARC LIGHT targets; COMMANDO NAIL (operations in which delivery of ordnance was accomplished by radar bombing) support with two-ship flights providing warning and direct suppression of SAM threats to single or two-ship COMMANDO NAIL missions; and IRON HAND Trail--day visual operations directed at searching or destroying SAM sites in a specified area.[10/]

Except for the normal problems encountered in night formation, darkness caused no significant en route problems during IRON HAND missions for flights of four or less aircraft. In fact, tanker rendezvous was often simplified at night. The advantage of having a second crewmember aboard was also apparent, since the pilot was not burdened with changing radio channels, operating navigational equipment and keeping a constant check on engine and flight instruments. Since COMMANDO NAIL missions were flown utilizing a single, or flight of two aircraft, problems due to darkness were minimized. Navigation was successfully accomplished in F-105s by use of their Doppler, TACAN, and Ground Map Radar Equipment.[11/]

Although neither type of the Wing's aircraft was equipped with terrain clearance radar, North Vietnam (NVN) defenses did not force night fighter-bombers to descend to an altitude where this equipment was required. Flights often operated at a minimum en route altitude (MEA) of 1,000 feet above the highest obstacle within three miles of course, and depended upon variations in altitude and routes to defeat early warning and height-finder crosstell. Enemy radar detection of incoming raids at night did not, in most instances, stimulate enemy defense reaction, as much as the actual weapon impact in the target area. On clear nights, a tactic used by pilots of the 388th TFW to combat the accuracy of enemy ground fire, was the brief use of afterburner, terminating it just prior to a major turning point. Another tactic, used with excellent results, was rapidly increasing altitude by four-to-five thousand feet just prior to starting the final bomb run.[12/]

Darkness imposed no serious problems or limitations on tactical reconnaissance aircraft, while en route to the target. The 460th Tactical Reconnaissance Wing (TRW) operated four types of aircraft: RB-57s, RF-101s, RF-4Cs, and EC-47s. Since the RF-101 was equipped with photo sensors only and did not carry precise navigation equipment, its reconnaissance mission was limited to daylight hours.[13/]

The RB-57 was not equipped with a sophisticated navigation system such as an inertial navigation system (INS) and mapping radars, but it did have a night optical capability (with use of photoflash cartridges) and the RS-10 infrared (IR) system which provided excellent imagery below 3,000 feet above ground level (AGL). Darkness created no serious en route problems for the RB-57 in good weather and over relatively flat terrain. The Real Time View feature associated with the IR sensor was used as a navigational aid; however, the altitude limitation of the RS-10 system restricted its night capability over mountainous terrain.[14/]

The sophisticated systems aboard the RF-4C minimized its en route problems and limitations due to darkness. Navigation was accomplished by INS, forward looking radar (FLR) and TACAN equipments. The combined use of these systems was generally adjusted for en route navigation to a preselected turning point or initial point (IP), for further egress to the target area.[15/]

The 432d TRW, flying F/RF-4s, experienced no serious difficulties en route to the target area. When TACAN was found to be weak and unreliable, the INS equipment was used with excellent results within its design limitations. Ingress to the target area was made at reasonably high airspeed, while avoiding known, antiaircraft artillery (AAA), and enemy positions.[16/]

Thus far in this discussion, the problems and limitations attributable to darkness were typical, more or less, of those encountered by units operating high performance aircraft. Many of these were also common to units operating low performance aircraft. Unique or special problems were encountered by units operating over a certain geographical area or performing a special mission. For example, the impact of darkness on the mission of the 21st Special Operations Squadron (SOS) was so severe that certain important operations could not be accomplished.[17/] The primary mission of the 21st SOS was the deployment of sensing devices in support of a highly classified project. The squadron also provided direct airlift support during infiltration/exfiltration operations of another sensitive project. Additionally, it was tasked with airlifting troops in the vicinity of Nakhon Phanom Air Base, Thailand. The squadron was equipped with ten H-3E helicopters.[18/]

The nature of the 21st SOS's mission was such that target areas had to be acquired visually prior to, and during, the delivery of sensors. Since these devices were deployed from treetop level up to 1,000 feet AGL, night/weather operations were not considered practicable. Infil/exfil operations were not attempted at night for the same basic reasons. In these operations, visual contact had to be established with the helicopter landing zones (HLZs), if the operation were to be successful. Under the conditions of darkness, this was almost impossible. Night operations were conducted in the immediate vicinity of the base. The purpose of these missions was to provide perimeter surveillance through use of Starlight Scopes, flares, and aircraft spotlights. Operations of this type proved to be highly successful.[19]

Darkness, combined with a hazardous operating area, created serious en route problems for the 22d Special Operations Squadron. The squadron's mission was night interdiction of truck traffic in the STEEL TIGER portion of Laos. In addition, the mission included night armed reconnaissance, close air support (CAS), and forward air controlling in the BARREL ROLL area of Laos (Fig. 2). The Squadron employed A-1E/H aircraft to perform these missions. Navigation en route to the target area was almost entirely dependent on TACAN or radar vectors from Ground Control Intercept (GCI) agencies. To a certain extent, pilotage was used during moonlight conditions; however, the extreme sensitivity of certain areas often made this technique unusable. Due to the hostile nature of the en route areas, most low performance aircraft, such as the A-1 and A-26, flew with the

FIGURE 2

aircraft blacked out. This required strict altitude control and radar monitoring to reduce the possibility of mid-air collision. The two factors considered most important from a flying safety point of view were the danger of mid-air collisions and spatial disorientation. Collision avoidance was considered a serious problem, because of the high density of night traffic operating below 10,000 feet AGL without position lights. The rugged terrain and rapid maneuvering associated with strike missions were found to be extremely conducive to spatial disorientation and vertigo. To minimize the hazards of these two problems, the 22d SOS stressed the need for a strict traffic control agency and the importance of pilots maintaining instrument flying proficiency.[20]

A situation similar to that of the 22d SOS existed in the northern Laos BARREL ROLL operating area of the 602d SOS. Utilitizing the A-1 series of aircraft, the squadron's primary mission was to conduct daylight strikes. However, sorties included strike, forward air control (FAC) escort for insertion/extraction of guerrilla teams, close air support, and armed reconnaissance of enemy controlled road segments. Occasionally, and generally in support of correlative night strike squadrons, pure night operations were undertaken. During these missions, the aircraft were configured with flares and ground markers at the expense of strike ordnance. The lack of reliable navigation aids was the single, most serious problem while ingressing to the target area. TACAN coverage in the BARREL ROLL area was meager at the time (only one station) and grossly unreliable. Radar assistance provided by EC-121 aircraft was utilized when possible and was accurate to within five miles.[21]

Darkness had a serious impact on Search and Rescue (SAR) escort missions. The squadron made several unsuccessful attempts to develop night SAR tactics. The failure was directly related to the inability of pilots to maintain visual contact with the rescue forces en route to, and over the survivor. A complicating factor was the rugged karst terrain and the necessity for operating at very low altitudes. Additionally, the SAR helicopter needed a horizon reference to hover, and its equipment was inadequate for use in performing that maneuver.[22/]

Darkness imposed various problems and limitations on the multiple operations of the 606th SOS. Equipped with two types of aircraft, the squadron was tasked with performing night FAC missions using C-123s, and psychological warfare and other related missions with U-10s. Darkness prohibited the U-10D aircraft from conducting its leaflet dispensing (LITTERBUG) and loudspeaker (LOUDMOUTH) missions. The U-10D had two limitations which precluded its operation in night/weather conditions. One was the lack of either TACAN or Search Identification Feature (SIF) equipment. Without these, there was no means of obtaining accurate position fixes during periods of darkness/weather. The other, and most important, was the U-10D was not equipped with suitable flight instruments to fly at night or in weather.[23/]

The C-123 (Candlestick call sign) was utilized for night reconnaissance of the route structure in central Laos, and as a forward air control (FAC) aircraft for interdiction strikes. Since the normal crew of seven included two navigators, no serious navigation problems were encountered en route to the target area. One navigator was responsible for directing the aircraft over the route structure, while the other navigator operated the Starlight Scope and provided navigational assistance as required.

During these operations, the 606th SOS Candlestick aircraft encountered a condition that may have been a greater hazard than AAA accuracy. It was caused by high intensity traffic in a relatively small working area, which greatly increased the potential of mid-air collision. In adjacent sectors were Candlestick (C-123), Nail (O-2), and Blind Bat (C-130) FACs, all working assigned strike aircraft. If the strike aircraft were fast-movers (jet aircraft), inadvertent overlap into an adjacent area often occurred during strike operations. This situation greatly increased the risk of mid-air collision, since all aircraft normally operated without lights.

Continuous efforts were made to reduce this risk and FACs were required to thoroughly brief all strike aircraft under their control of the status of operations in nearby areas. Overlap rarely occurred when strike aircraft were slow-movers (conventional aircraft). GCI stations attempted to provide information, but at times, their capability was limited by the large volume of traffic. Area assignments and tactics to correct these conditions were constantly coordinated with controlling agencies. Good results were obtained by establishing buffer zones between sectors, improving the scheduling of FAC aircraft to prevent excessive time-on-target overlap, and by improving communication between FAC aircraft.[24]

Several other units were concerned about the dangers involved while operating in high density traffic areas. One of these was the 609th SOS, with the primary mission of night interdiction of the enemy's line of communications (LOC) from North Vietnam, through Laos, into South Vietnam. The squadron was also called upon to provide CAS for friendly forces under enemy attack. These two missions were accomplished with A-26A aircraft. The 609th SOS made the following comment on the potential danger of mid-air collisions:[25]

> *"The biggest problem encountered by A-26 crews while en route to the target area is the mid-air collision potential. We climb to and cruise at between 7,000 and 9,000 feet en route to the target and at this altitude are always subject to enemy ground fire from AAA positions. Consequently, we cannot turn our navigation or rotating beacon lights on at night. The mid-air potential is reduced through positive control of our air traffic. Initial night operations used altitude separation as the primary means of control, with TACAN/DME to aid in fixing ground positions. Radar has been incorporated into this system and now adds positive lateral separation. This problem begins en route to the target but continues through every other phase of the mission."*

The high density of air traffic ingressing (and egressing) the target area at night was considered by the 8th TFW to be a significant problem, especially when the aircraft were blacked out due to the enemy's defensive threat. Although this problem was somewhat relieved by airborne radar,

24

the 8th TFW believed that the real answer was strict command and control by Airborne Battlefield Command and Control Centers (ABCCC) and Combat Reporting Centers (CRC), and judicious scheduling to preclude oversaturation of target areas.[26]

F-100 pilots of the 35th TFW encountered similar problems due to high density traffic, while flying CAS missions. Many pilots experienced near misses with the FAC or Flareship.[27] Frequently, during immediate scrambles to support troops in contact with enemy forces, the FAC was unable to effectively perform his enormous task, which included briefing strike pilots on the pattern of the Flareship, establishing restricted run-in headings, coordinating with ground units, and working the fighters. This condition contributed to the possibility of mid-air collisions.[28]

A final example of the inherent risk of mid-air collisions during night operations, was the experience of the 8th Tactical Bombardment Squadron (TBS). Equipped with B-57s, the mission of the 8th TBS was night interdiction against supply and infiltration routes leading into South Vietnam (SVN), and providing close air support and target destruction as requested. Reduced visibility due to darkness was the basic problem en route to the target area. Although GCI provided traffic advisory service, the probability of mid-air collision increased proportionally with the increase in numbers of aircraft in the area, and as saturation of GCI was approached. At the time, the 8th TBS aircraft maintained visual meteorological condition (VMC) **quadrantal** separation altitude, but the pilots were totally responsible for the avoidance of other aircraft.[29/] To reduce the danger of mid-air collision, the 8th TBS stated a preference for treating all night flights in accordance with instrument meteorological condition (IMC) procedures, with hard altitudes assigned to all aircraft operating above a specified flight level.[30/]

Flight C of the 5th SOS was a Psychological Air Warfare unit based at Binh Thuy AB in the Mekong Delta region of SVN.[31/] Utilizing U-10Ds and C-47s, its mission was the daytime dissemination of leaflets over specified targets and conducting day and night propaganda broadcasts. Because of the navigation and flight instrument limitations of the U-10, it was not used on night missions. Some of the C-47s were equipped with TACAN, which was used to get the aircraft to the target area without serious problems. TACAN, however, was not accurate enough to put the aircraft precisely over the target and visual references had to be used. In aircraft not equipped with TACAN, the pilot had to maintain visual contact with the ground all the way en route to the target. During missions without moonlight, the aircraft was navigated to the target by TACAN or pilotage. Once over the target area, the pilot put the aircraft into an orbit, and with the assistance of the navigator, attempted to locate the exact target. When proceeding to the next target area, time and heading were flown and the process was repeated.[32/]

Summary

The severity of the impact of darkness on the en route portion of the mission profile was dependent upon several factors; such as, nature of the mission; type aircraft; operating area; and pilot experience. Some of the most serious problems included flight join-up, inadequate aircraft lighting systems, danger of mid-air collision, and spatial disorientation. Of these problems, several prevailed in weather conditions as well.

Problems and Limitations Attributable to Weather

Weather not only increased the number and seriousness of en route problems and limitations, it often caused missions to be diverted or even canceled. As in darkness, one of the aspects presenting a serious problem was the formation join-up. Sometimes it was more feasible to use radar assistance and delay the join-up until the aircraft were in VMC, either between cloud layers, or on top of clouds and overcast. Usually, flight to the target area was accomplished under one of these conditions. The main exception was when thunderstorm activity presented an inpenetrable barrier across the route of flight. Generally, these storms could be circumnavigated visually or by means of ground or airborne radar. During solid weather conditions, most flights remained in close formation or moved into in-trail formation by using airborne radar, such as that in F-4Ds.[33/]

The performance limitations of the F-100, with a full load of fuel and ordnance, presented a special problem during join-up and ingress to the target area under IMC.[34/] After takeoff, 60 miles were covered during the climb to an optimum cruise altitude of 15,000 feet. With triple

27

ejector racks installed, and a few more bombs, the optimum cruise altitude was reduced to 13,000 feet, while the climb distance increased to about 70 miles. During the climb to altitude, pilots had to effect a join-up, while flying a heavily loaded aircraft which had very little power to spare. During the monsoon seasons, the same lack of power often forced the F-100 to fly at lower altitudes, or under complete instrument conditions.[35/]

When ceilings were minimum IMC, VMC, the cloud tops were above the service ceiling of the aircraft, join-up could be extremely hazardous. A procedure used by F-100 pilots of the 37th TFW, in lieu of marginal weather join-ups or separate aircraft proceeding long distances in search of a clear area, called for formation takeoffs. This technique reduced the possibility of mid-air collisions, due to unknown closure rates and restricted visibility.[36/]

The impact of weather was a serious problem during all phases of a mission, and as might be expected, its limitations varied in relation to a unit's mission and operating environment. The 355th TFW considered weather the greatest single influence in successfully accomplishing its mission. During IMC departures, the takeoff interval for the Wing's F-105s was increased, delaying join-up and completion of visual checks of each aircraft to determine if ordnance had been lost during takeoff or climb. During the spring season, thunderstorms often forced strike aircraft to deviate from their planned route. Tanker aircraft were required to change their scheduled air refueling contact point (ARCP) to permit the strike force to join-up in favorable weather conditions. This change caused additional flight planning computations for the strike crew and, when executed during the force type mission, made it extremely difficult for the flights to rendezvous at a preplanned position. When the tanker drop-off was changed due to weather, the F-105 strike force commander had no adequate means to update the Doppler for accurate navigation and, unless a visual or TACAN fix could be obtained, it could result in navigational errors up to several miles. Impact of this error was the difficulty experienced in correcting back to the desired track. Due to the structure of the force, corrections had to be small, because an increased angle of bank degraded the force's electronic countermeasure (ECM) capabilities. One solution to this problem was to request the airborne radar control ship to provide vectors to place the force back on course. [37/]

COMMANDO CLUB missions (COMBAT SKYSPOT release in NVN) were seriously affected by adverse weather. Due to the surface-to-air missile (SAM) threat, adequate separation from clouds was required to provide visual detection of launched missiles and enable strike crews to take evasive action. When aircraft could not remain at least 8,000 feet above an undercast and 3,000 feet below an overcast, while operating between a minimum of 13,000 feet to a maximum ceiling of 17,000 feet (for F-105 aircraft), the mission had to be aborted. Visibility for missions in NVN was required to be at least five miles. [38/]

En route weather created several common problems for the pilots of the 388th TFW. Other problems were directly related to a particular type mission. En route thunderstorms forced all aircraft to deviate from course. Heavy weather cells were successfully circumnavigated by using airborne radar; however, the intensity of some cells caused a "radar shadow", which made it very difficult to positively identify areas of hazardous weather. Rendezvous with the tanker in the cumulus buildups was virtually impossible. One solution, which was not always possible with the F-105D/F, was to climb and make the join-up on top of clouds. Fortunately, outstanding coordination between GCI and the tanker aircraft usually made it possible to find and remain in clear areas, until refueling was completed.[39/] Because attack courses were carefully preplanned and studied, and compensating for deviations in course was difficult, thunderstorms between the IP and bomb release point presented a serious problem for COMMANDO NAIL operations. The 388th TFW proposed:[40/]

> *"The solution to this problem is very precise and reliable navigation equipment, accurate to within 2,000 feet, which would allow flexibility in approaches to the target or precise return to original ingress route after deviations to avoid weather build-ups."*

Weather created some of the most difficult problems in flight join-ups of the 31st TFW. Similar to those encountered at night, join-ups consequently were not made before reaching VMC. Instrument departures were made under radar control; however, the local radar approach control (RAPCON) often lost contact with the flights within 15 to 20 miles from the base. Once the flights were joined up, the only problem was avoiding an occasional thunderstorm.

Weather also presented problems after reaching the target area. When arriving over the target area under IMC, the letdown to VMC altitude was dependent upon the nature of the local terrain and the height of overcast. When an IMC letdown had to be made without navigational aids, the procedures used by the 31st TFW were to descend to 2,000 feet above the highest obstacle within 25 miles. An alternate method, preferred by most pilots, was to find a clear area for descent and then fly VMC to the target. When neither of these methods was practicable, flights executed a standard instrument approach at the nearest navigational facility and then flew VMC to the target area.[41/]

Pilots of the 8th TFW encountered problems similar to those of other strike aircraft. A join-up technique, made possible by radar capability of the F-4D, was that of flying radar-trail until reaching VMC. When VMC could not be attained, join-ups utilizing aircraft and GCI radar were made as a last resort. The 8th TFW, as well as other units, experienced excess static on the UHF radio, while flying in weather. Often this condition made communications marginal, if not impossible. A problem, unique to many of the sophisticated missiles and weapon systems employed by the 8th TFW, was encountered while flying through precipitation. Under this condition, the sensitive, glass seeker-heads of these weapons were very likely to be damaged. Examples of affected systems were the AGM-62 Walleye, the AIM-9 Sidewinder, and the Paveway Laser-Guided Bomb.[42/] The 8th TFW was not the only unit to express concern over this problem. Freezing temperatures, as well as visible moisture, may have had some adverse effects on various weapons and weapon fuzes. These conditions were often encountered during climb and descents to and from higher altitudes. The 366th TFW thought it possible that some of the dud ordnance, which had been attributed to unknown causes, may have been due to icing. It was the Wing's opinion that studies in this area should be made, especially on the FMU-56 radar fuze and raw air-dispensed weapons. 43/

Enemy defenses presented additional problems for aircraft flying in weather conditions in the vicinity of SAM threat areas. As mentioned previously, a visual missile sighting capability was required as a defense against SAM attack. This requirement could not be compromised. Weather further degraded the SAM acquisition capability of F-4 aircraft Radar Homing and Warning (RHAW) equipment by causing erroneous indications. Therefore, special emphasis was placed on the importance of maintaining a visual sighting capability in these areas. 44/

Weather was a far greater impediment to reconnaissance operations than was darkness. Occasionally, when weather conditions were below takeoff minimums, missions were canceled. If weather forced returning mission aircraft to land at an alternate air base, valuable time was lost in the interpretation of exposed film. Inclement weather had a serious effect on the capability of airborne equipment. All imagery, including IR and radar, was seriously degraded by visible moisture between the aircraft and target.

To effectively employ any of their sensors, reconnaissance aircraft assigned to the 460th TRW were not equipped with terrain avoidance radar. The lack of this equipment made it difficult to safely descend through weather over mountainous terrain. Under these conditions, the crew normally made descents over water or areas of known, level terrain, and then flew VMC, low-level approaches to the target, frequently in a hostile environment. When the target area was mountainous, and the peaks were obscured by clouds, it was often impossible to acquire the target. The RF-4C was more versatile under similar weather conditions, because of its terrain avoidance radar capability. 45/

The unique mission of the 460th Tactical Reconnaissance Wing's EC-47 aircraft was seriously impaired by en route weather. During these missions, it was necessary to visually acquire known checkpoints about every 20 or 30 minutes to reset the Doppler navigation equipment for maximum accuracy. This was normally accomplished with a driftmeter. However, it frequently became "fogged up" for varying periods of time, when the aircraft penetrated areas of visible moisture. The presence of heavy moisture also weakened the Doppler return signal, which in turn, degraded navigational accuracy.

Thunderstorms had a strong impact on the accuracy of EC-47 Airborne Radio Direction Finding (ARDF) equipment. When areas of severe or extreme turbulence were encountered, navigators and radio operators were unable to perform their mission. Consequently, most ARDF operations were conducted VMC on top; however, the lack of pressurization and oxygen equipment limited the EC-47 to an altitude of not more than 10,000 feet. The professionalism of the EC-47 aircrews enabled them to partially overcome many of the limitations imposed by weather. Loran "C" equipment did not prove to be acceptable and, although the installation of Loran "D" was being considered, what was really needed, in the opinion of the 460th TRW, was an electronic method of setting the Doppler with an accuracy to within one-tenth of a mile. 46/

Pilots of the 432d TRW were also concerned with the inability of their RF-4 sensor equipment to penetrate weather. Additionally, the narrow search scan of the terrain following radar, did not show sufficient clearance to the side of the aircraft. 47/

Slow-movers, such as the A-1s of the 1st SOS, had some advantages while operating in poor weather conditions. When the unit was performing the role of close air support in SVN, there was little, if any, heavy antiaircraft opposition, and the A-1 could operate and survive under low ceilings. The slow speed and small turning radius of the aircraft made it possible to keep the target in sight even during low visibility conditions. TACAN fixes, UHF-DF and FM-DF were used to locate FACs and friendly ground positions. When the 1st SOS moved to Nakhon Phanom AB, Thailand, weather became a more significant factor, because the operating environment of Laos was much less permissive than that of SVN. In addition, the Squadron's primary mission was changed to include interdiction, helicopter escort, and mine dispensing. In this environment, the slow speed of the A-1 severely restricted its use in areas where the enemy employed 37-mm AAA weapons. These areas had to be overflown at high altitudes, or else completely avoided. Unfavorable weather conditions with extensive cloud conditions often limited or forced the cancellation of all missions. A unique problem was encountered by the 1st SOS during periods of heavy rainfall. Excess drainage often caused the aluminum matting of the temporary runway at Nakhon Phanom to be undermined. When this occurred, the runway had to be closed for repairs, and takeoffs and landings were made from a parallel taxiway. Under these conditions, landing minimums were greatly increased because GCA precision approaches could not be utilized. 48/

Summary

A highly important aspect of weather operations in SAM, MIG and AAA threat areas, was that defense against these weapons was practically impossible; thus, air operations of all aircraft in such an environment were severely limited. 49/ Weather caused the cancellation of certain types of missions: LITTERBUG and LOUDMOUTH missions were not flown in weather by C-47s assigned to C flight, 5th SOS. The high density traffic in the Mekong Delta area, combined with en route navigation limitations, made instrument flying hazardous and was not done. 50/

When en route segment of the mission profile was conducted during weather conditions, the problems and limitations encountered by aircrews definitely increased. As in the case of darkness, join-ups, formation flying, spatial disorientation, and mid-air collisions were areas of real

35

concern. In addition, weather made navigation more difficult, had adverse effects on aircraft equipments, and severely limited operations in high-threat areas. Most important, it could cause the cancellation of critical air operations.

CHAPTER III

IMPACT OF DARKNESS AND WEATHER
ON TARGET ACQUISITION PROCESS

The success or failure of a mission was largely dependent upon the ability of the aircrew to acquire the target; either visually, electronically, or with the aid of ground/airborne radar. Darkness and weather, or a combination of both, made the target acquisition process one of the most difficult and demanding phases of the mission profile.

Problems and Limitations Attributable to Darkness

Visual acquisition of targets during darkness was a difficult task even under ideal conditions. When other factors such as rugged terrain, spatial disorientation, high density traffic, limited fuel supply, and enemy defenses were added, it became a formidable task. In addition to the problems involved in pinpointing the exact location of a target with the aid of FACs, illumination and ground markers, the success achieved in acquiring a specific target was also dependent upon its characteristics and geographical location. The performance capabilities of the aircraft employed were also an important consideration.

Locating point targets was best accomplished by thorough, premission planning and precise en route navigation, utilizing ground/airborne radar and aircraft navigational systems. Once in the immediate area, specific targets could be visually located by moon/starlight, flarelight, FAC, or combinations of these methods. Moving targets, such as trucks, presented more of a challenge. While moon/starlight provided sufficient illumination to see such targets, it also allowed vehicles to operate blacked-out, greatly compounding the problem of visual acquisition. Dark nights required trucks to operate with lights and provided strike aircraft with a definite advantage. Twilight scopes, IR detectors, and high resolution radar were used successfuly in initially locating specific targets and targets of opportunity.[1/]

Even though a FAC, or member of the strike flight, could identify a target and possibly illuminate it, the problem often became one of communication between the FAC and strike aircraft. Once flares were dispensed, trucks immediately took cover. To reacquire a target of this type, FACs had to provide strike aircraft with precise information on its new location. If this information were not, or could not be provided, the enemy's trucks and supplies were very likely to escape destruction.[2/]

A proper flare dispensing technique was a critical factor in visually locating a target. Although a tremendous light source, flares were not effective, if they were poorly placed or dropped too high or low. Terrain haze, cloud ceilings, and run-in headings were all important factors, but if flaring was not accurate, effective ordnance delivery was not possible. It was also important to keep constant flarelight on the target. A loss of target illumination wasted precious time in re-flaring and reacquiring the target. Highly experienced night crews, accustomed to working together, were probably the best means of overcoming these problems.[3/]

The least demanding missions, so far as target acquisition was concerned, were COMBAT SKYSPOT. On these missions, pilots dropped their ordnance at the direction of ground radar controllers and were not particularly concerned with actual target acquisition. On the other hand, NIGHT OWL missions were extremely demanding and target acquisition was a most important aspect of the mission, especially when flown in close support of troops. 4/

During most NIGHT OWL missions flown by F-100 pilots of the 31st TFW, target acquisition was dependent upon flare illumination and proper flare positioning. On close air support missions, absolute identity of the target was mandatory and flares were always used. Interestingly, in the Korean War, the Marines flew many CAS missions at night without the aid of flares. Pilots were able to identify the respective forces by alignment of gun flashes and make accurate attacks against enemy positions. 5/

Pilots of the 35th TFW also put great emphasis on the importance of proper flare quantity, positioning, and timing. In their experience, best results were obtained when at least three flares were burning at all times; properly spaced, and positioned evenly to one side of the target and parallel to the final run-in heading. This technique provided adequate illumination for identifying general features of the target. 6/

The 2.75-inch white phosphorous marking rocket was not considered suitable for night operations. When the pilot's attention was diverted from the immediate target, such as during a cross check of engine and flight instruments, there was a good chance that he would fail to notice the ignition of the marking rocket upon impact. If the flash of ignition was not observed, the resulting smoke quickly disappeared and became indistinguishable from smoke created by illumination flares, making target acquisition extremely difficult. What was needed, according to the 35th TFW, was a bright, long-burning marking flare capable of being delivered with the 2.75-inch rocket.[7/] Although illumination flares were adequate for most night operations, several units thought the overall quality could be improved by incorporating design changes which would permit launch from a higher altitude, delayed opening capability, chute collapse after burn-out, and improved descent stabilization.[8/]

Target acquisition posed several serious problems and limitations for B-57 pilots of the 8th TBS. Generally these problems could be separated into two categories: target area location and specific target identification.[9/] Rules of Engagement required that all visual strikes flown by the 8th TBS be conducted under FAC control. Normally, the FAC provided strike aircraft with a TACAN/DME fix from a certain TACAN station by using a map overlay or indications from TACAN equipment. This fix was used to accomplish rendezvous with the FAC. Because of the FAC's relatively low altitude over the extremely mountainous terrain of the infiltration routes leading into SVN, maintaining TACAN lock was sometimes difficult and made fixes unreliable. The impact of this situation was that strike aircraft consumed valuable time and fuel in the general vicinity of the target prior to locating the FAC or target. Shielded, rotating beacons on some FAC aircraft were helpful but were of little value, unless fixes were accurate enough to get strike aircraft into the FAC's immediate area. Flare illumination was excellent for locating a target area; however, against trucks it compromised the element of surprise. Problems and limitations falling into the category of target area location would have been minimized if air-to-air TACAN and the ARA-25 (VHF-DF-HOMER) had been installed in both the strike and FAC aircraft.[10/] Pinpoint identification of a specific target within the target area was a difficult problem, and imposed the most serious limitations on the 8th TBS's night operations. Although there were some disadvantages in using flares when attacking trucks, the 8th TBS found they could be used very effectively to acquire targets such as roads, fords, stalled vehicles, and slow-moving watercraft.[11/]

Some problems inherent in the use of flares were almost impossible to overcome. Flarelight tended to blind the aircrew or obliterate the target during the final run-in, causing inaccurate delivery or dry passes. The swinging action of flares during descent greatly increased ground glare and caused moving shadows. Each of these conditions could cause loss of target or disorientation. Flares, especially when used below an overcast, were advantageous to enemy defense in tracking attacking aircraft.[12/]

The use of ground markers for target acquisition eliminated many of the disadvantages of air-launched flares. However, in mountainous or forested terrain they were difficult to see from all angles. Also, it was always possible that the enemy would counter the effects of ground markers by lighting decoy fires. Occasionally, red-burning markers were used. These markers were superior to the white marker because of their distinct color, longer-burn duration and higher intensity.[13/] The primary disadvantage of ground markers was that they were difficult to deploy with accuracy. In high AAA threat areas, the FAC had to drop them from a relatively high altitude, making them subject to wind drift during descent. It was not unusual to have a marker placed 500 or 600 meters, or more, from the specific target. In this event, the aircrew was faced with the problem of estimating the exact location of the target.[14/]

A tactic used by an 8th TBS pilot was to drop one napalm on the spot where the aircrew believed the target was located, and then have the FAC give offset corrections from the napalm fire in terms of azimuth and napalm fire widths. As primitive as this method was, it proved to be surprisingly effective, even against moving targets. A drawback to this tactic was that B-57s carried only four napalms and in using one to mark targets, depleted 25 percent of their napalm capability.[15/] Further, it was not always feasible for strike aircraft to carry their own flare illumination. For example, carrying flares on the F-100 resulted in the loss of two ordnance stations, and degraded the range as well as the ordnance load.[16/]

An operation in which some rather unique problems and limitations were encountered during target acquisition was Operation COMMANDO SABRE. COMMANDO SABRE (CS) began in July 1967 and was conducted by the 37th TFW. In this operation, F-100F aircraft were used as Forward Air Control vehicles

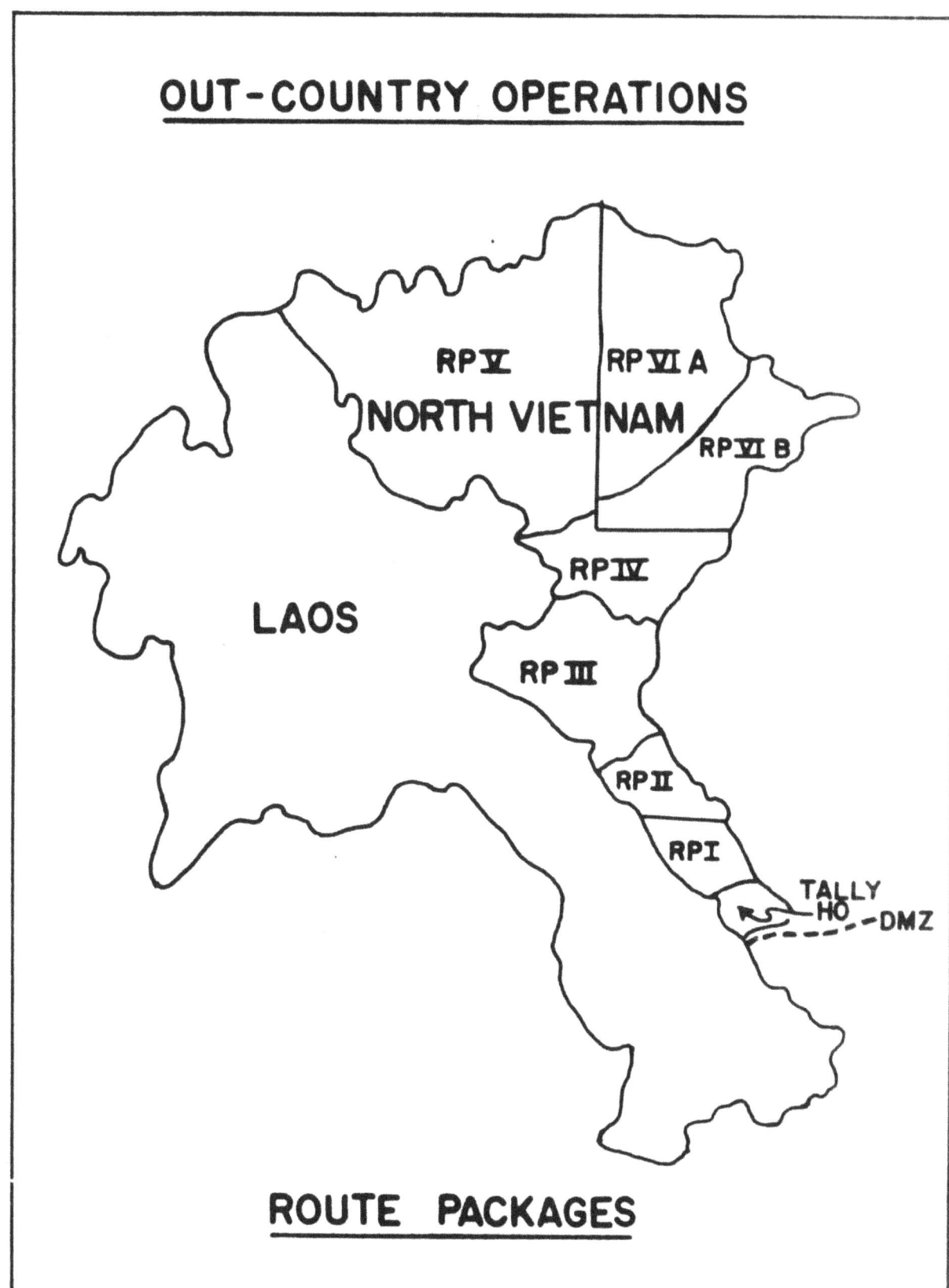

FIGURE 3

in Route Package I (RP-I) of North Vietnam and several areas in Laos.[17] (Fig. 3.) In July 1968, COMMANDO SABRE was a test program to evaluate the effectiveness of high speed aircraft in the role of night, visual reconnaissance, and forward air control in RP-I. The F-100F aircraft were configured with standard illumination flares and an AN-PUV-3 Starlight Scope. During this phase of CS, intelligence information was gathered; however, successful control of airstrikes was quite limited.[18]

Little success was achieved during the four months of CS night operations for several reasons. First, the F-100F did not have the capability of remaining on station for a sufficient period of time to effectively conduct visual reconnaissance in forward areas. On a typical four-hour mission, a great portion of the allotted time was spent en route to and from the home base or tanker refueling tracks. On the average, the en route portion of the mission consumed up to two and a half hours of flight time, thereby reducing time on station to between one and two hours. Secondly, an accurate target marking device for the F-100 was not available. Long-burning flares, used late in the program, could not be dropped with any consistent accuracy to pinpoint target locations. In addition, the element of surprise was compromised by flares, and moving traffic either drove out of the flarelight or headed for shelter, compounding the target acquisition problem for the strike aircraft. Another handicap in locating targets was the fact that the F-100F did not carry enough flares to put continuous illumination on a target. A total of only eight separate flare drops could be executed. This limited supply was totally inadequate to do the job. Finally, only one flight of strike aircraft could be cleared into the target area at one time because of the danger of mid-air collision between the blacked-out aircraft. This limitation, combined with the problems of target acquisition, aircraft pattern spacing, and the requirement to interspace flare deliveries between ordnance passes, drastically reduced productive time of the F-100F on station.[19]

Many other difficulties were encountered, which severely limited effectiveness of F-100Fs in the role of a night reconnaissance and FAC aircraft. Not least among these was the AN-PUV-3 Starlight Scope, which was too long and bulky to be used effectively in the relatively small cockpit area of the F-100F. Because COMMANDO SABRE operations had not proved very effective, except for limited success in visual reconnaissance and intelligence gathering, they were suspended.[20]

Other jet fighter aircraft carried their own flaring capability. The F-4C/D was capable of carrying a total of 64 MK-24 flares through use of the SUU-25/A Dispenser. The dispenser contained four tubes, each capable of receiving two flares, with a total of eight flares per dispenser. A minimum of two flares was released each time a dispenser tube was activated. The authorized flare load consisted of eight SUU-25/A dispensers, two on each outboard station at the aft Multiple Ejector Rack (MER) position, two on the centerline station at the aft MER position, and one on each inboard station Tank Ejector Rack (TER). The MK-24 flare, depending upon MOD, burned from 150-180 seconds and produced illumination rated at 2.0 million candlepower. Approximately 15 seconds were required for flares to reach maximum intensity after ignition. A nominal value for flare coverage was a circle with a one nautical mile diameter. Flares were normally set to burn out at approximately 500-1,000 feet AGL. Once the target had been located, the lead aircraft made a rapid climb to the best flare altitude and released flares. In the case of the normal 20-second ejection and ignition settings, the altitude was 5,000 feet AGL, 450 KCAS, and in level flight. In a typical armed recon mission, a two-ship flight would enter the target area maintaining trial formation with a 4-6 NM separation. After the lead aircraft dispensed flares, the number two aircraft began to attack the target. Alternating attacks were then continued by lead and number two aircraft. If required, the lead aircraft would reflare the target and attacks continued.

Of all the problems associated with night target acquisition, the two most common among all operational units were those of target illumination and marking. Even during twilight hours, target acquisition created problems. The 355th TFW was normally not tasked to support the night interdiction program, except for occasional night COMBAT SKYSPOT missions and twilight, visual dive bombing. The lengthy shadows and reduced visibility during the twilight mission made target identification extremely difficult for the Wing's F-105 pilots. Most of these missions were usually located along narrow, dirt roads, only 10-12 feet in width. Under these conditions, it was mandatory that the proper sight picture be obtained as a near-miss did little, if any, damage to the target. Because of the difficulty of target identification and sight alignment during these periods of reduced light and visibility, the Wing requested that its strikes be terminated at sunset and not begin again until after sunrise.[21]

Units which were more specialized in conducting night strike missions and utilized late model aircraft, equipped with sophisticated navigation and weapon systems, were not exempt from the problems involved in night target acquisition. One of the units in this category and equipped with F-4D aircraft, was the 366th TFW. There were two areas in the night target acquisition process, which the Wing considered to be of major concern-- initial location and marking of the target, and inadequate intensity of illumination flares. For locating the target, the 366th TFW expressed the need for a navigation system with an error no greater than one nautical mile per hour of flight. The Wing's F-4D Inertial Navigation System generally accrued an error of at least two-to-three miles during one hour flight. A more accurate INS would have allowed aircrews to mark or illuminate a target by using the Weapons Release Computer Set (WRCS) in conjunction with radar "show", offset aim point. With a precise navigation system, illumination could also have been accomplished visually by illuminating an offset aiming point (OAP), located five-to-ten miles from the target. This flare light could then be used to position the aircraft exactly over the OAP. The "freeze" and "insert" functions of the WRCS would then be activated and an accurate flare drop could be made over the target, utilizing the offset bomb mode.[22] Another factor which complicated flaring a target was the high susceptibility of the Log and MK-25 flares to wind effects. This decreased the accuracy in placing a flare directly over the desired point.[23/] In the opinion of the 366th TFW, the flares in use did not provide sufficient illumination to enable adequate detection of pinpoint targets. Log flares, used by FACs for ground marking, could seldom be seen above 12,000 feet AGL; they were not easily discernible from fires already burning in the target area. The MK-24 flares did not burn with sufficient intensity to illuminate small targets, so they could be detected by the aircrews at, or near, the desired roll-in altitude. This forced the pilot to descend to acquire the target and increased the chance of his losing it as the aircraft climbed back to the desired roll-in altitude. Maneuvering also reduced the useful flare illumination time, and induced a hurried roll-in and delivery by the aircrew.[24/]

As mentioned earlier in Chapter II, the 388th TFW conducted three distinct missions. Target acquisition presented different problems in each of these roles. Normally, the 388th TFW did not conduct night strikes. When these missions were conducted, it was usually done under flare illumination. Since the problems of acquiring targets under these conditions were similar to those of other units, they need no further discussion at this point. However, the Wing's EF-105F pilots used a different technique for acquiring targets. Target acquisition by EF-105F IRON HAND aircraft was accomplished electronically, which presupposed an active SAM threat. Tactics were based on maintaining immediate proximity to known SAM sites, by reference to Doppler and TACAN equipment, while maintaining a readiness to fire an AGM-45 (SHRIKE), if a threat which provided valid SHRIKE guidance should occur. To provide maximum mission and mutual support, two Wild Weasel aircraft were employed against each selected SAM site. Utilizing this technique for target acquisition, darkness was of little consequence.[25/] COMMANDO NAIL operations presented no serious target acquisition problems when radar scope photography was available and navigation as accurate to within one mile. These missions were analogous to day visual strike and successful target acquisition required detailed study of the target as well as precise navigation.[26/]

Reconnaissance aircraft were confronted with several problems which were unique to the night reconnaissance mission. The most serious problem in target acquisition was the lack of visual identification of the target. It was further compounded by the fact that the majority of night reconnaissance targets were area coverage and LOCs. The Vietnamese topography presented its own limitations. Characterized by either vast flatlands of the Delta regions or mountains of the highlands, there were few targets which could be accurately identified in darkness, either visually or with FLR.[27/] As a solution to target acquisition problems/limitations, an identifiable IP was selected and the run-in and target acquisition were made by precise control of heading, airspeed, and time. Due to mission requirements for operating at a relatively low altitude, and the resulting degradation of radar returns at these altitudes over many areas of Vietnam, these IPs had to be either a coastal point or some other prominent radar return with a run-in from IP to target of up to 40 miles. En route from the IP to the target area, maximum advantage was made of radar returns, INS, and TACAN. When possible, multiple IPs and run-in headings were planned for operational flexibility.[28]

Target acquisition for slow-movers, such as A-1 and A-26 aircraft, was generally not as difficult as it was for fast-movers. For both types of aircraft, success in acquiring a target was directly proportional to the quality of target illumination and the FAC's ability to describe the location of the target in relation to visible reference points.[29] Visually acquiring the target during darkness required either moon/starlight, flare illumination, or ground markers. Colored pyrotechnics were best suited for ground markers, although fires from previous strikes could also be used. When using only ground markers, the actual target to be struck was often not visible and in reality, was only a point in darkness, referenced to the visible markers.[30]

In all night operations, an important flying safety aspect was knowing the exact position of the aircraft at all times. In some operational areas, targets were often surrounded by sheer karst formations, towering four-to-five thousand feet above the strike area. The karsts were difficult to see at night and their tops were often obscured by clouds. Shadows cast by flares and reflections from clouds, produced an environment conducive to spatial disorientation. Under these conditions, it was absolutely essential that aircrews be highly competent instrument pilots.[31]

Reliance on TACAN fixes to effect rendezvous between strike and FAC aircraft was mentioned previously as being a limitation in the night target acquisition process. Due to the combined, inherent inaccuracies of airborne TACAN receivers of two different aircraft, A-26 pilots of the 609th SOS experienced serious difficulties in locating FACs. In fact, it was not unusual for A-26 aircrews to conduct strikes having only voice contact with the controlling FAC. Although shielded, rotating beacons were helpful, the 609th SOS emphasized the need for a more reliable system to expedite rendezvous. Flares were sometimes used by FACs to assist in making rendezvous. As mentioned previously, the obvious disadvantage in this procedure was that it provided the enemy with ample warning of the impending airstrike. On a clear, moonlit night, target acquisition was naturally simplified, and few serious problems were encountered, because terrain features were fairly easy to distinguish.[32]

From its extensive night operational experience, the 22d SOS concluded the two most significant lessons learned were: first, there was no substitute for aircrew proficiency in night/weather instrument flying; and secondly, there was no substitute for flying a well-planned strike, without unnecessary haste.

Two urgent requirements needed to improve the utilization of the A-1 (or similar) aircraft at night were noted by the 22d SOS. The first was

50

improved navigation equipment, such as Loran D, to overcome the deficiencies experienced with TACAN at low altitudes and long distances from the station. The second was an improved communication system, incorporating a secure voice capability. With the equipment available at the time, serious problems were encountered in maintaining communications with control agencies, when operating at low altitudes and at long ranges. Lack of secure communications meant that the lone pilot of a single engine, heavily loaded, unstable aircraft, had to divert his time and attention to encode/decode vast amounts of information. [33/]

Performing night reconnaissance and acting as FACs for strike aircraft in the route structure of central Laos, the C-123 Candlestick aircraft from the 606th SOS were an integral part of the target acquisition process. Because of their long endurance, capability to carry large loads of flares and markers, and stability as sighting platforms, the C-123s were well-suited for the job. [34/] Target acquisition was accomplished primarily with the Starlight Scope, which was manned by one of the two navigators aboard. The two loadmasters were responsible for dispensing flares and markers. When the Starlight Scope operator acquired a target, it was marked with three MK-6 ground markers, deployed in a line relative to the target. Instructions to the strike aircraft were then given in terms of distance and bearing of the target from one of the three markers. Occasionally, MK-24 flares were used to illuminate a target. Flare illumination, however, proved less satisfactory than markers, because it removed the element of surprise and illuminated the strike aircraft, increasing its vulnerability to enemy AAA. [35/]

The tactic most successfully employed by A-1 pilots of the 22d SOS was that of working with a FAC who, with the aid of a Starlight Scope, searched the area for targets. This technique required the long fuel duration of the A-1, plus a great deal of patience on the part of the crew.[36/]

A common complaint voiced by aircrews from almost all units, regardless of the type of aircraft flown, was directed against inadequate interior light systems. Not only was this deficiency considered a flying safety factor, but it interfered with target acquisition. The lack of proper light intensity controls required crews to carry rolls of tape to cover those lights which impaired their night vision.[37/]

Summary

The target acquisition process during hours of darkness was one of the most critical and essential elements in the entire mission profile. Certain problems and limitations involved in target acquisition were applicable to almost every operational unit, regardless of its mission, while other difficulties were mission/aircraft peculiarities. The success of target acquisition during the hours of darkness was, to a large degree, directly proportional to the difficulties experienced in locating the immediate target area and the quality of illumination and ground markers put on a specified target.

Problems and Limitations Attributed to Weather

Several factors governed the force of impact which weather had on the target acquisition process. Of these, terrain in the target area, existing weather, and aircraft/weapon systems capabilities were among the most significant. Night weather conditions either made visual target acquisition impossible (or at least, not feasible), or very difficult as well as hazardous. Few strike missions were conducted without visual reference to the target. Those that were flown under complete IMC, or above an overcast, were normally made by using airborne radar on ground radar control, such as COMBAT SKYSPOT.

Once over the target area, a decision as to whether the target could be visually acquired and attacked, had to be made. Weather permitting, an attempt was made to acquire the target visually. If weather prevented visual attacks, there were several alternatives available: proceed to secondary targets; conduct COMBAT SKYSPOT strikes; use airborne radar to locate and strike target; or as a last resort, abort the mission and return to the base without expending.[38/]

Generally, weather over the target area provided one of two situations. Either low stratus overcast conditions, which denied the vertical for maneuvering prevailed, or cumuli prevented strike aircraft from taking advantage of a variety of run-in headings.[39/] Target acquisition under a low ceiling or low visibility was sometimes extremely difficult, especially under the latter condition. Normally, before an attempt was made to locate the target, it was first necessary to locate the FAC. If the target area were in mountainous terrain, high speed maneuvering, while seeking or keeping the FAC in sight, could be extremely hazardous. Low visibility added to the problem of sighting the target, because the white smoke from the FAC's marker was indistinct in the haze and could easily be confused with smoke from previous strikes or other areas. Under these conditions, colored smoke, used for marking positions of friendly troops, was also difficult to spot.40/ When working in daylight, on top, and through low, scattered, or broken conditions, visual contact with the target was often lost, because the white marker smoke was easily confused with low, white clouds. Under these conditions, colored marking rockets were a definite advantage.41/

Target acquisition boiled down to the problem of getting the strike aircraft in position to attack, and then identifying the target to the strike pilot so he could deliver ordnance. In the case of trucks, most were sighted by FACs, with and without the aid of sensors. Targets lost to weather were an indication of the lack of an all-weather capability. Seventh Air Force believed that the first significant in-theater improvements that might have been obtained in instrument weather strike capability, was the Tropic Moon III (B-57 aircraft equipped with Low Light Level Television). Meanwhile, it was necessary to exploit the limited all-weather capability of sensor-equipped or slow-speed attack aircraft to the greatest extent possible.42/

All units unanimously agreed there was no substitute for flying a

54

ALPHA STRIKE FORCE TEAM

AIRCRAFT	NUMBER	MISSION
F-105D/F-4D	16	Strike
F-105F	8	SAM/AAA Suppression
F-4C/D	8-12	MIG-CAP
EB-66*	6	ECM
KC-135*	16-21	Tanker
EC-121*	3	MIG Warning
HH-3E/HH-53B*	3	SAR
A-1E*	4	SAR Escort
C-130*	2	SAR Support
TOTAL	66-75	

* These aircraft remain on-station to support two strikes.

FIGURE 4

well-planned strike, without unnecessary haste if good results were to be expected. The available time on station determined how much time could be devoted to acquiring and attacking a target. The F-4, operating at a 200-NM range, had only about 20 minutes loiter time before having to expend ordnance (which took about another 20 minutes). If air-to-air refueling were available, the time could be extended 40 minutes, to an hour. The A-26, by contrast, could remain on station almost five hours at 200-NM. The A-1 and B-57 could remain on station about two and a half and one and a half hours, respectively.[43/]

The Alpha Strike Force, based in Thailand, but under operational control of 7AF, flew 96 percent of the USAF attack sorties flown in the high threat areas of NVN (RP V and VI) in 1967. A typical breakdown of the aircraft by type, number, and mission necessary to support the force package for one strike is shown in Figure 4. The Strike Force Commander was responsible for navigation to the target and for leading the formation into the dive bomb run on predetermined attack directions. He was also responsible for coordinating with tanker forces to affect massing of the entire strike force for pre-strike refueling, ultimately arriving at the northern tanker drop off point with all flights in visual contact with each other. The commander arranged his flights into a box formation with each flight in pod formation (flight leader forms his flight in "normal formation" with 500 to 1,000 feet lateral and vertical separation), and the flights themselves positioned in proximity to each other, offering mutual ECM protection.

The most critical point in force-type missions like those conducted by the 355th TFW, was target acquisition. Therefore, weather was a most important consideration. Unless the force commander was able to navigate exactly to the proper roll-in point, at least 10-to-15 miles were required to realign the force, so as to reach the exact roll-in point. Where more than three-eighths cloud cover existed, this was often not possible.[44/] When strikes were conducted in low-threat areas, with individual flights or aircraft, weather became a less important factor. Weather criteria in this instance were determined primarily by aircraft performance, and whether target identification was made by a FAC or the pilot of the strike aircraft. When a FAC was available, strike aircraft could operate under ceilings of 8,000 feet and visibility not less than three miles. During periods of low visibility, the normal target acquisition procedure used by the 355th TFW, was for the Flight Leader to descend, acquire, and strike the target. After his strike was completed, the remaining flight members made their descent and hopefully, were able to use the impact of the leader's ordnance for an aiming point.[45/]

If the weather forecast indicated marginal weather in the target area, strike aircraft having an offset bombing capability, such as the F-4Ds of the 366th TFW, had to be prepared to acquire the target and deliver ordnance, either visually or by offset bombing, utilizing the WRCS.[46/] A major factor, which had a direct bearing on the degree of success attained in locating targets during marginal weather or night conditions, was the extent of the aircrew's personal knowledge and familiarity with the target area. This factor was an important reason the majority of the Wings preferred a **specific operating area of respon**sibility be assigned each wing.[47]

Since IRON HAND missions involving SHRIKE launches used electronic means for acquiring targets, weather was not a serious problem. However, when making visual attacks during search and destroy operations, it was desirable to have a ceiling of 10,000 feet and five miles visibility for target acquisition and maneuvering.[48] During COMMANDO NAIL operations, weather was only a serious problem when thunderstorms or numerous, small weather cells were located in the vicinity of the target area. Where thunderstorms were shadowing or otherwise obscuring the radar aiming point, there was no way to insure accurate target acquisition and ordnance delivery. Although less serious, weather cells had a tendency to obscure radar returns, which served as pointer systems used to help identify the radar aiming point. With the exception of these conditions, weather was generally considered advantageous to COMMANDO NAIL missions, because it tended to lessen flak reactions.[49]

The terrain avoidance radar of the RF-4C aircraft enabled it to acquire targets denied other reconnaissance aircraft. Nevertheless, low ceilings frequently prevented even the RF-4C from acquiring needed intelligence. Combined with darkness, there was always a good chance that the target could not be acquired.[50] RF-4C aircrews were constantly faced with the problem of acquiring a target with pinpoint accuracy by use of FLR and associated INS. The primary limitation in the FLR was the lack of an integrated electronic crosshair, which could be moved with a tracking handle. The only offset capability at the time was a rather antiquated range course cursor, which had no tracking capability. Urgently needed was an electronic crosshair, controllable with a tracking handle, and tied into the INS to provide tracking/offset information. Operating in III and IV Corps (Fig. 5) areas of SVN and specifically, along the Cambodian border, presented a real challenge to the radar operator, since there were few usable radar returns in these areas. An improved FLR with serviceable crosshair/offset capability would have made it possible to use these same returns with increased accuracy in target acquisition. This was but one example of several improvements which were needed to enhance the night/weather capability of the RF-4Cs.[51/]

The primary mission of the 553d Reconnaissance Wing (RW) was to provide airborne monitor of sensor emplacements in order to collect and relay this information to Task Force Alpha in support of the IGLOO WHITE sensor system. Equipped with EC-121R aircraft, the 553d RW maintained around-the-clock orbital platforms in certain, designated areas. Color designators were used to identify different orbital areas.[52/] During the 1967-1968 period, the 553d RW averaged about 3,025 flying hours per month. Approximately 20 percent of this time was under IMC, including the en route and on station time. Icing and thunderstorms were of major concern to aircrews; however, weather also had adverse effects on the ground-placed acoustic and seismic detection

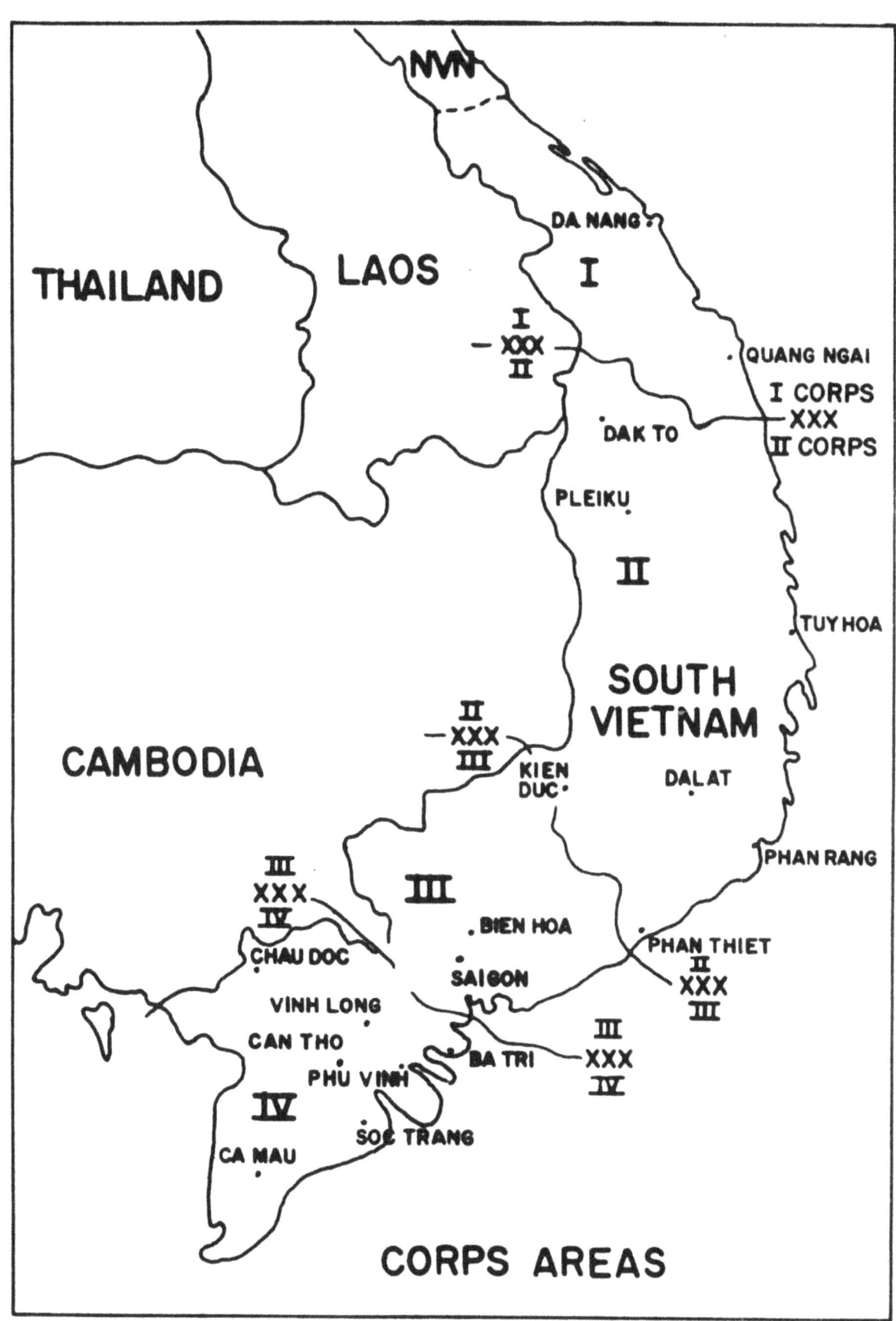

FIGURE 5

sensors.[53]

The Acoustic Detection Sensors were affected in two distinct ways. First, they were activated by non-threat noise sources such as heavy rain, running water, high wind, and thunder. The non-target noise detection of vehicles was almost impossible due to the audio camouflage they created. Secondly, a single acoustic detection sensor picking up weather-generated noise, effectively eliminated valid target sounds transmitted by any other sensor on the same frequency (channel). It was possible for heavy rain to cause one sensor to mask valid target noises from 26 sensors located in other areas.[54] Seismic Infiltration Detection sensors were relatively immune to adverse weather. Thunder was capable of significant, invalid sensor activation. However, the activation did not interfere with other sensors on the same frequency. Hourly weather reports, relayed to the Infiltration Surveillance Center (ISC), enabled its personnel to anticipate weather effects on the sensors and were an aid against mistaking spurious activations for target activity.[55]

Severe weather also had detrimental effects on the EC-121R aircraft. Continuous operation in heavy weather and icing, caused serious damage to the nose radomes in unanticipated proportions. For example, during "Typhoon Bess", 24-hour station coverage was maintained by EC-121R aircraft but, the nose radomes were eroded to the point of having to be replaced. Thus, the supply of radomes was exhausted in a short time.[56]

Summary

The impact of weather on the target acquisition process was serious during periods of unfavorable weather involving low ceilings or visibilities; it completely negated the possibility of visual target acquisition. Even if the target could be acquired during marginal weather conditions, it was often lost because of low ceilings/visibilities before ordnance could be delivered. Furthermore, there was not an aircraft in SEA, which had a weapon system capable of acquiring pinpoint targets in an all-weather environment. Because of these limitations, weather forced strike aircraft to use an alternate means, such as COMBAT SKYSPOT or airborne radar, for area target acquisition. As will be seen in Chapter IV, the accuracy with which ordnance could be delivered was basically dependent upon the aircrew's ability to visually acquire the target.

CHAPTER IV

IMPACT OF DARKNESS AND WEATHER
ON TARGET ATTACKS

Many of the problems encountered during the target acquisition phase extended into the attack phase. Rather than reiterate these, emphasis in this chapter is directed toward ordnance delivery, achieving accuracy, and tactics and techniques, especially COMBAT SKYSPOT, used to counter effects of darkness and weather.

Problems and Limitations Attributable to Darkness

In view of the difficulties and hazards associated with conducting strikes during periods of darkness or weather, it is well worthwhile to look at some of the flying safety aspects of these missions prior to addressing the intricacy of the attack phase itself. Flying safety was a major concern during all combat operations. During night or weather conditions, the utmost caution had to be exercised by supervisory and aircrew personnel. One of the most important measures taken to insure safety, as well as effectiveness, was through mission planning. This was best accomplished with prebriefed and fragged areas/targets. An exhaustive study to gain a thorough knowledge of terrain, landmarks, LOCs, and enemy defenses was an absolute necessity. A review of 1:50,000 charts, recent area photographs and mosaics, and current intelligence reports on area defenses had to be accomplished, and in most cases, committed to memory. Best possible attack headings and run-in lines had to be determined and aircraft performance and limitations considered.[1]

Vertigo or spatial disorientation was an ever-present problem during night/weather operations, because of the lack of a visual horizon. Adding to this problem, was the "milk bowl" effect encountered under flare flight, and flying in and out of clouds during ordnance delivery and pullout. These two conditions were particularly conducive to vertigo.[2] From a flying safety aspect, aircraft with two or more crew members were better suited for the night/weather strike mission, because the additional crewmember could monitor the position/altitude of the aircraft, relaying as necessary, corrections or information to the pilot. This allowed the aircraft commander to concentrate on acquiring the target, positioning the aircraft for attack, and visually tracking for ordnance delivery.[3] It was imperative that the pilot maintain a knowledge of his exact position at all times when operating in rugged or mountainous terrain. In addition, he had to be able to recognize his own limitations as well as those of the aircraft. If the situation ever arose which was beyond his capabilities, he was expected to use good judgment, and if necessary, return to the base without having expended ordnance.[4]

In SEA, advances in night delivery of weapons were made in the field of training and indoctrination of aircrews. Upon arrival in the theater, crews inexperienced in night combat tactics, often voiced doubts that night delivery of ordnance could be done either accurately, safely, or orderly. After undergoing intensive training programs and building up their night flying proficiency, they soon lost those doubts.[5/] Often the Wings were burdened with the job of training newly assigned aircrews, who had no previous experience in tactical fighter wings, and were inadequately trained for night and instrument flying. Some graduates of Replacement Training Units (RTU) were simply not given ample opportunity to develop their proficiency, nor did they seem to be impressed with the fact that night and instrument flying were routine aspects of the fighter pilot's mission.[6/] One condition precluding some Wings from maintaining a high degree of proficiency in night operations, and making it impracticable for them to establish a night-dedicated squadron, was their being fragged with only four to six missions per night.[7/]

In describing the problems associated with night attacks, the 8th TFW probably expressed the feelings of all fighter pilots on the subject in the following words:[8/]

> *"The prime problems of the attack phase at night consists of attempting to maintain target acquisition and orientation while performing high "G" maneuvers looking directly into bright flare light or at a dimly visible ground area. This is undoubtedly one of the most dangerous aspects of night combat. Vertigo and spatial disorientation are constant threats."*

In the early stages of night operations in SEA, most night strikes were carried out with four aircraft formations. Through the experience gained as operations progressed, it was found that smaller size flights were more ideally suited for night operations in the SEA environment. Flights consisting of two aircraft were more easily managed during night and minimum weather conditions. Many targets apparently did not require the ordnance loads carried by more than two aircraft. By reducing the number of aircraft on a target, more targets could be struck with the same number of aircraft. Generally, most units utilized the two-ship flight, or even single ships. Flexibility was retained, however, and larger size flights were utilized when required.[9/]

Delivery accuracy at night depended to a great extent on the type ordnance used. Low drag bombs, for example, required dive tactics and high roll-in altitudes, which greatly increased the problem of keeping the target in sight. In addition, bombs were a poor area coverage weapon. Targets of opportunity, such as "movers", presented themselves more at night, but they also represented a smaller aiming point. A truck visible at 3,000 feet completely disappeared above 7,000 feet. Destruction of a truck with an MK-117 bomb required a hit within 25 feet. Few pilots were able to achieve that accuracy, particularly at night. Area weapons such as Cluster Bomb Units (CBUs), napalm, rockets, and 20-mm cannon, which were delivered at lower altitudes and shorter slant ranges, greatly improved accuracy and mission effectiveness.[10/]

One of the greatest deterrents to accurate weapons delivery at night in the F-4D was the excessive switch changing required to select various weapons. This problem was aggravated by inadequate cockpit lighting and armament control panel location. This problem was peculiar not only to the F-4D, but was a common gripe among pilots flying all types of aircraft.[11/]

The steep dive angles and high speeds used by 355th TFW F-105 crews in dive bombing, were compromised by the reduced flight visibility and depth perception encountered in twilight/night attacks. In most cases, pilots were unable to distinguish the target, until the release parameters were realized. Reducing the dive angle resulted in increasing the slant range distance, which further hampered proper tracking as well as exposing the aircraft to a hostile ground environment for a longer period of time. To complicate matters, the gun sight of F-105s could not be properly dimmed for night operations and adversely affected the pilot's night vision. The degree of accuracy achieved during periods of darkness was difficult to determine because sufficient light was not available to record results on strike camera film.[12/]

Problems and limitations encountered by the 355th TFW in night attack operations were primarily due to avionics of the Wing's F-105s being designed for nuclear delivery; they did not provide the accuracy needed for conventional weapons delivery during night/weather conditions. None of the aircraft assigned to the 355th TFW had been modified to accomplish the night/weather bombing mission, as had the F-105 (COMMANDO NAIL) aircraft assigned the 388th TFW.[13/]

Night attacks by F-105 IRON HAND aircraft of the 388th TFW consisted only of SHRIKE launches at an electronic threat. On one or two occasions, when SHRIKE impact resulted in a fire, limited efforts were made, with doubtful success, to deliver 20-mm cannon fire from high angle and high altitude (6,000 feet AGL), into the fire area. A SHRIKE launch generally resulted in the immediate shutdown of SAM guidance signals and this satisfied the IRON HAND mission requirements.14/

The 388th TFW favored the two-ship flight on all strike missions. At night, all aircraft usually carried at least two CBU-24s with Fuze Munition Unit (FMU) fuzes for use in flak suppression. Firing of the internal gun was limited to two second bursts when possible, to minimize exposure to enemy fire.15/

Flying safety precautions were stressed by all units, however, the possibility of flying into the ground was one of the most dangerous aspects of night operations. Collision with the ground may have contributed to more combat losses than any other factor. Recent experience indicated that this problem had been minimized by precautionary rules/procedures such as those implemented by the 8th TFW. These measures included:16/
(1) Using experienced aircrews with a detailed knowledge of the target area terrain along with selected crews specializing in delivery of certain types of ordnance such as CBUs; (2) Never attacking unless there were a visible horizon, or the target were illuminated by flare light, moonlight, or ground light source; (3) Reemphasizing the importance of having the

pilot closely monitor altitude and rate of descent during the attack; (4) Never assuming that aircraft position was known, and never penetrating an undercast or letting down to an unsafe altitude on a dark night; and (5) Using all available navigational aids and continually cross checking one against the other, because a one-mile navigation error could very well have meant the difference between a successful mission, or an abrupt bash into a karst ridge. Innovations such as these, used in conjunction with tactics manuals developed by each tactical fighter wing in SEA, greatly enhanced the overall effectiveness of night combat operations.[17/]

As mentioned several times previously, the problem of spatial disorientation or vertigo was ever-present during night operations. Extra caution was required while executing the attack phase, because the rapid change of lighting conditions when pulling off the target subjected the pilot to a disorienting environment, making an instrument recovery necessary. At times, flares became positioned directly between the roll-in point and the target. This created a blinding effect during the attack and made transitioning out of the bright flare light abrupt and difficult, and resulted in late target acquisition.[18/]

Dive deliveries initiated above flare altitudes, posed a unique visibility problem. As aircraft approached altitude of the flare, it entered into an apparent haze layer. This problem was reduced by offsetting flares and releasing ordnance above or below the burn height. When properly deployed, flares burned for approximately 1,300 feet of fall and would normally burn out about 1,000 feet AGL. As the flare burned, it caused a subdued light directly beneath it. For this reason, and to allow for possible ignition failures, a minimum of two flares were normally dropped on each flare drop pass. If both ignited, the separation caused by ballistic and fuze tolerance resulted in an overlap of flare light, which in turn, brightened the area of reduced intensity directly beneath each flare.[19/]

In high threat areas, the 37th TFW found that battle damage was greatly reduced by keeping operating time below 4,000 feet AGL to an absolute minimum. This meant restricting ordnance loads to those which allowed recovery with minimum time below 4,000 feet AGL. Consequently, known high threat areas, such as Lower Route Package and Laos, were fragged for low drag ordnance only. There was one exception: CBUs delivered in Laos and Lower Route Package by the Wing's F-100s at an altitude of 500 feet AGL. The normal procedure employed for this delivery was to acquire the target, without alerting the enemy if possible, and then making one high speed (500 kts) delivery pass releasing all CBU ordnance.[20/]

The Dive-Toss mode of delivery used by F-4 pilots proved to be highly effective for night operations, and under most conditions would effect a more accurate weapons placement than the visual bombing system. Because of the inherent inaccuracy of night deliveries, regardless of the system used, area coverage weapons such as the CBU-24, CBU-2, or the SUU-23s

(Suspension and Release Units, used in conjunction with the F-4D Lead Computing Optical Sight System) decreased the need for pinpoint accuracy.[21/]

The urgent need for a more effective area coverage weapon was further stressed by the 8th TBS. Achieving "pinpoint" accuracy at night with the delivery system of B-57s was very difficult. Even so, the results obtained were surprisingly good, probably because of the high experience level of the squadron's pilots. The 8th TBS believed these results could be dramatically increased through use of an area weapon such as the M-35 or M-36 incendigel cluster bomb. This bomb would cover an area approximately equivalent to a football field. Any vehicle or personnel lying within this coverage would very likely be destroyed by the ensuing fire. The increased size of the destructive area of the weapons would also compensate for some of the problems of target acquisition and accuracy of delivery. Although the standard BLU-27 napalm was effective against vehicles and personnel, the area coverage was only about one-quarter that of the M-35/36 and required more precise delivery.[22/]

The 8th TBS was operating on the outer fringes of its aircraft range capability. Any holding that was required in the target area (holding was normally required), reduced the available time for working the target. By hurrying ordnance delivery to maintain adequate fuel reserve for return flight to the base, not only decreased the target destruction probability, but increased the chance of pilot error and vertigo. It should be noted that this problem was encountered not only by the TBS, but several other units as well.[23/]

Equipment limitations were responsible for some of the problems encountered by the 432d TRW, while conducting night reconnaissance missions. Due to the relatively low intensity of the photo flash cartridges, sensor operation had to be conducted at lower altitude limits. This limited target coverage and placed the aircraft well within the range of hostile fire. A higher intensity cartridge would have increased target coverage and reduced vulnerability of the aircraft to enemy fire. Also needed, according to the 432d TRW, was the addition of 6-inch oblique cameras to the current configuration of one 6-inch, nose vertical, and two 6-inch split cameras. This modification would have provided greater target coverage, while allowing crews to obtain information from an offset position.[24/] By increasing the capabilities of IR and Side-Looking Airborne Radar (SLAR) equipment, so that intelligence could be gathered without the use of photoflash cartridges, crew survivability in hostile areas would have been greatly enhanced. The 432d TRW thought this capability would have been ideal for use against LOC type targets.[25/] Finally, the 432d TRW was against the employment of reconnaissance aircraft on night, airborne alert, because they believed safety hazards involved in flying at low altitudes in mountainous terrain without prior detailed flight planning outweighed the intelligence information obtained.[26/]

Conventional aircraft encountered the same type of problems, although perhaps not as critical, as did jet aircraft. The A-1 pilots of the 22d

70

SOS utilized standard daytime ordnance delivery techniques for night deliveries. The danger of spatial disorientation during dive bomb recoveries and evasive maneuvers was considered to be a serious problem. Consequently, great emphasis was placed upon relying on flight instruments to effect recovery. From the Squadron's experience, accuracy of ordnance delivery was limited most of all by the directions received from the FAC, or in other words, target acquisition. When the target was a moving truck, the FAC was not sure what its position would be at the time the strike aircraft attacked. If the errors induced by lack of precision in locating the target were removed, the accuracy achieved in darkness was comparable to that of daylight deliveries. According to the 22d SOS, the most significant lesson learned from its extensive night operations was no substitute existed for good instrument flying, or for flying a well-planned strike without unnecessary haste.[27/]

The A-1 pilots of the 602d SOS were in complete agreement with the 22d SOS on the subject of instrument proficiency. In addition, they stressed the importance of maintaining proficiency in close, night/weather formation flying. Two squadron aircraft were saved during the last rainy season, after experiencing complete instrument failure, because the pilots were able to stay in formation until making a safe landing. On another occasion, an aircraft was lost due to instrument failure at night. The 602d SOS believed a superior and effective night reconnaissance capability could be achieved by use of a tracking, low light level sensor, coupled to a level bombing computer and release system similar to that used in Tropic Moon II aircraft (B-57s equipped with Westinghouse Low Light Level

Television weapons delivery system).[28]

Darkness did not cause any unique problems for A-26 crews of 609th SOS, although aircraft limitations did have some adverse effects on delivery accuracy. High altitude (5,000' AGL) ordnance release was used against targets such as supply depots and trucks in the Ho Chi Minh Trail area to minimize exposure to ground fire and insure safe terrain clearance. Bombing from this altitude did affect accuracy somewhat, because most of the time the target could not be seen and strikes had to be directed at a reference point on the ground. In addition, at 5,000 feet AGL the mil depression of the A-26 bomb sight was such that the crew could not put the pipper on the target at the desired release point. Consequently, the crew had to rely on feel and judgment and make an estimate of the correct release point. An improved bomb sight would certainly have enhanced the 609th SOS's night bombing capability.[29]

A common problem encountered by A-26 crews when working with flares, was that of avoiding burnt-out flares and chutes. Often, as many as a dozen burning flares, plus an unknown number of expended flares, were over the target area at the same time. Several methods were used as a solution to this problem. First, all passes were made so as to always remain above the flares. The disadvantage of this method was that it decreased delivery accuracy. However, the alternative of going under the flares was certainly not recommended in high threat areas. Another method was used when the FAC had the capability to drop low-burning flares. In this case, flares ignited at about 1,000 feet AGL and burned all the way to the ground. If the FAC was able to place the flares close enough to the target, this was an acceptable method and also decreased the problem of vertigo and spatial disorientation.30/

Problems and Limitations Attributable to Weather

Weather in Southeast Asia was a major factor influencing combat air operations, and normally, mission profiles were determined by existing or forecast weather conditions. Weather was also a prime consideration in determining ordnance delivery with visual reference to the target, or by other means such as COMBAT SKYSPOT or airborne radar. It was also an important factor in determining the type of ordnance to be loaded on the aircraft.

Visual Attacks

Weather, such as low cloud decks, seriously hampered delivery patterns and occasionally precluded attacks. Bombing through or beneath a cloud deck also increased the possibilities of short rounds, low blows (self-inflicted battle damage), battle damage, and flying into the ground. However, these problems were not insurmountable, as evidenced by the many thousands of sorties successfully flown beneath 2,000-3,000-foot ceilings.31/

Working under a low ceiling or in low visibility definitely increased the difficulty of attacking a target; however, the degree of difficulty depended upon the type of ordnance carried. Loads which could be delivered at low angles of attack, such as napalm and high drag bombs, were most easily delivered. Even slick bombs, which were normally dropped in high-angle, were delivered under ceilings as low as 2,000 feet AGL by using bunt techniques or low-angle dives.[32/]

Although excellent accuracy could be achieved, working under low ceilings increased the dud rate and incidence of low blows. When fired at low angles, rockets were especially susceptible to causing damage to the delivery aircraft. Recovery from these deliveries required a sharp pull up to avoid the bomb frag pattern of a slick bomb and often carried the aircraft into the clouds or overcast, making it necessary to execute an instrument recovery and letdown back to VMC. Strafing was accomplished under low ceilings without difficulty if the target could be acquired.[33/]

Strike aircraft operating under low ceilings were particularly vulnerable to enemy ground fire and only under conditions of utmost urgency could the risk of attack be justified.[34/] In some areas, the inherent risk involved in low angle deliveries during night/weather conditions was too great to be acceptable. For this reason F-100s of the 37th TFW were restricted from making them in the high threat areas of Laos and the Lower Route Package.[35/]

To enhance the pilot's capability to cope with low ceilings, the 3d TFW urged the certification of high drag bombs, which were in use at the time, for cockpit selectable, high or low drag delivery. Although it was possible to load MK-82 (Snake Eye) and M-117 (retarded) bombs on the F-100 in this manner, it was not authorized.[36/] During operations affected by weather, extra caution had to be exercised to prevent the possibility of a short round incident. Low ceilings, with a commensurate short target acquisition time, resulted in a situation where the pilot was most exposed to a short round delivery.[37/]

Weather complicated the target acquisition process. In addition, a system for marking the exact position of a target was not available. What was needed, according to the 37th TFW, was an expendable, air-delivered, radar transmitter marking device, which would allow accurate weapons delivery through weather, if placed on the target by a FAC or other means. An aircraft with an attack and terrain avoidance radar, coupled with the radar marking device, should prove to be a highly effective weapon system.[38/]

In marginal weather conditions, maintaining sight of the target, or orientation with respect to the target, was difficult. Additionally, it affected the actual conduct of battle; i.e., how to avoid the gunnery range rectangular pattern and deny the enemy the knowledge of run-in headings. In each of these problems, pilot experience yielded its own solution. Two techniques for maintaining orientation were popular with F-4 pilots of the 8th TFW. The first was referencing relative to a prominent landmark; and the second was cranking the WRCS distance to zero and "inserting" while passing directly over the target. This technique provided direct read-out of bearing and distance to the target when the INS mode was selected.[39]

To insure flexibility in the conduct of battle, aircraft frequently worked the target individually. In this instance, the holding aircraft orbited high and was sufficiently displaced from the target area to afford complete freedom of movement to the attacking aircraft. Another technique was to use teams which continually flew together. Through experience, these teams developed the coordination which allowed them to attack simultaneously from random headings.[40] During daylight hours, it was best to make the minimum number of passes possible, for it was an acknowledged fact that survival potential decreased rapidly as the number of passes increased. This was especially true when operating under an overcast.[41]

Changing bomb run parameters; i.e., 30-degree versus 45-degree dive angle, due to adverse weather conditions resulted in decreased accuracy of delivery. The rapid mental calculations required to adjust the mil settings were often inaccurate due to changing the flight path to avoid clouds as well as rapid, last minute corrections to tracking when the target became clearly visible. Many of the targets hit by F-105 pilots of the 355th TFW were bivouac areas located in heavily wooded terrain and were very difficult to acquire in conditions of low visibility.[42]

The requirement for making continuous sight adjustments during run-in was eliminated by a locally developed modification to the 355th TFW's

F-105 gunsight. This modification provided a continuous solution sight, which permitted the pilot to align the aircraft in azimuth and disregard the dive angle (to the extent bomb flight time was sufficient to arm the bombs), and release the armament when the sight pipper passed through the target. With this system, the pilot was given great latitude in varying attack parameters. 43/

The combination of weather and SAM threat created a major defensive problem for IRON HAND (EF-105F) aircraft. Apart from the strike force pod formation, the only effective defense against a launched SAM was visual acquisition, because if they could not be seen, they could not be dodged. A minimum of 7,000 feet altitude was required for detection, decision-making, and evasive maneuvering to avoid a SAM. Because the loaded F-105F had an effective maneuver ceiling of approximately 17,000 feet, the 388th TFW believed that operations in a SAM threat area should be restricted to conditions where cloud tops were not above 10,000 feet. Haze conditions over North Vietnam often extended up to 14,000 feet or above. For all practical SAM evasion purposes, heavy haze had to be treated with the same respect accorded clouds.

In high threat areas, it was necessary to maintain a lateral separation of at least three miles from cumulus buildups. The axiom of staying at least 3,000 feet below a ceiling applied to SAMs as it did to AAA fire, because aircraft had been hit by SAMs that were arcing down. It was the 388th TFW's opinion that the importance of adequate separation from weather during anti-SAM operations could not be overemphasized. In addition, the Wing agreed with the supposition that since development of the Wild Weasel equipment and tactics employed at the time, all IRON HAND losses to SAMs occurred during violations of these weather criteria.[44/]

Weather imposed serious restrictions on the delivery of one of the most sophisticated weapons used by the Air Force in SEA. Paveway was the name used to identify the MK-84 (2,000-lb) and MK-117 (750-lb.) bombs, which had been modified with laser guidance kits. Delivery of Paveway laser guided bombs required considerable skill and training and the use of two aircraft. The first bombs were delivered by F-4 aircraft in the RP-I area between 22 May and 9 August 1968. One F-4 was equipped with a laser illuminator mounted on the rear canopy rail. The illuminator aircraft accompanied the attack aircraft and flew in an arc 12,000 feet above target. The illuminator pilot manually aimed the laser source at the target, while the bomb was delivered by the attack aircraft (Fig. 6). To provide an accurate source of guidance, the target had to be illuminated by laser energy more or less continuously, until weapon impact.

Tactics called for using roll-in from approximately 20,000 feet AGL, 45-degree dive, and release at approximately 12,000 feet AGL. Weather and ceilings below 14,000 feet AGL interfered with this tactic, because the target could not be illuminated. Weather conditions favorable to such tactics existed in RP-I about 25-to-40 percent of the year. At the time,

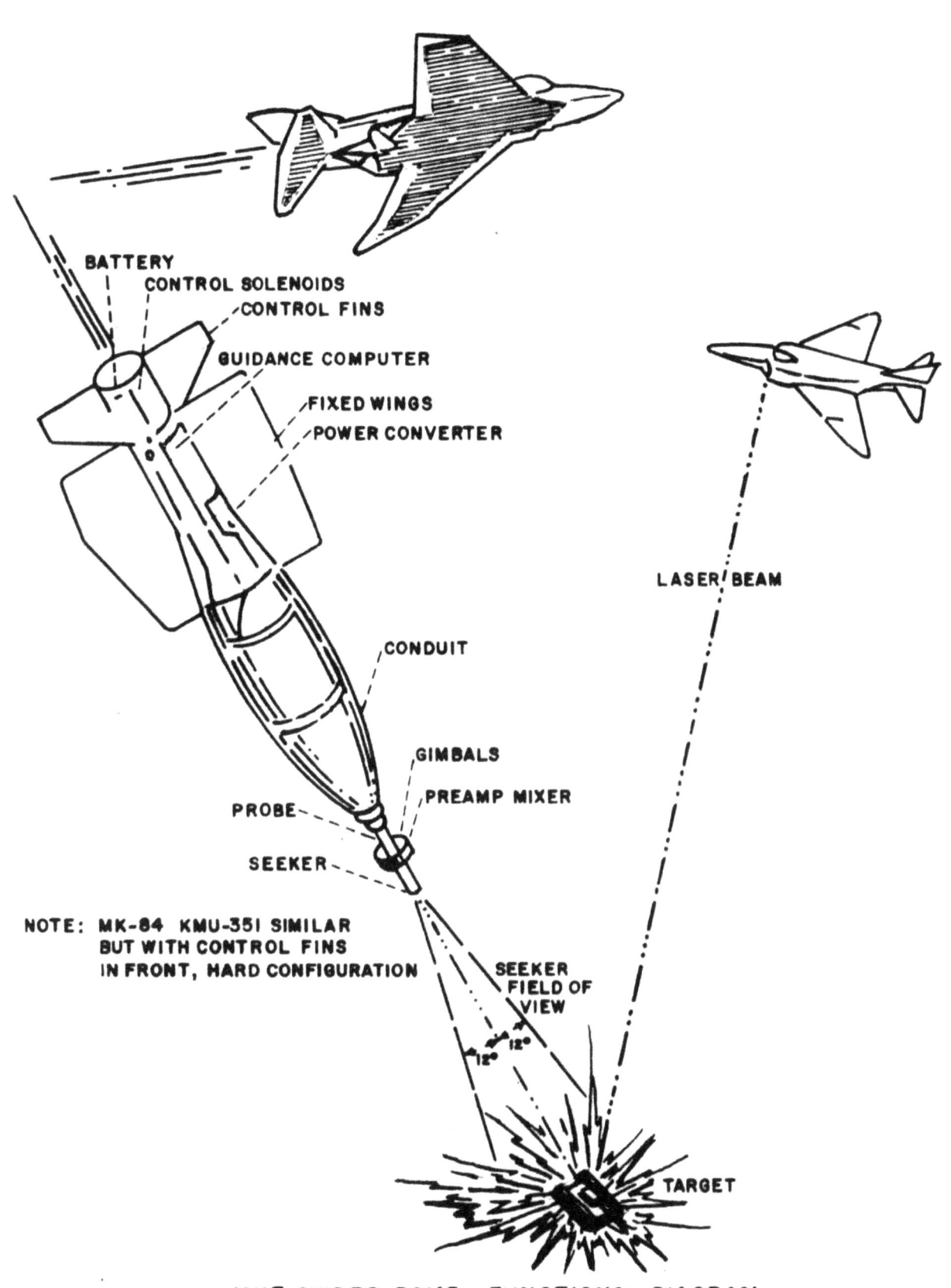

M117 GUIDED BOMB, FUNCTIONAL DIAGRAM

FIGURE 6

use of the laser guided bomb system was limited to day VMC. However, the design of the system did have a potential for developing a night capability. Use of the system at night with flare light or Starlight Scope in parallel with the laser marker was thought to be worthy of investigation. On one occasion, the seeker heads on four bombs were destroyed when the aircraft flew for approximately two minutes through heavy rain. 45/

Summary

At the time of this report, unfavorable weather precluded the delivery with any consistent accuracy, of ordnance by the aircraft/weapon systems employed in SEA. The impact of adverse weather on air operations depended upon its exact nature. It could be expected to affect, in varying degrees, important factors such as: tactics; flexibility of target and ordnance selection; maneuvering parameters; delivery accuracy; and vulnerability to enemy defenses. The aspects of flying safety were greatly influenced by weather conditions and made a dangerous job even more hazardous.

COMBAT SKYSPOT (MSQ-77)

The MSQ-77 equipment consisted of a pencil beam, X-Band radar, which operated most effectively in conjunction with an aircraft-installed SST-181 X-Band beacon. This beacon received, amplified, and returned the MSQ-77 signal. As a result, the capability and range of the COMBAT SKYSPOT system were greatly increased. The SST-181 beacon, in conjunction with the long-range modification on the MSQ-77 radar, increased the control range capability to 196NM. If a beacon were not installed in the aircraft, or if the beacon were inoperative, a skin paint method could be used as an alternate. Using this method, the effective range was reduced to 40-50 NM.[46/]

In SEA, the MSQ-77 system was utilized by tactical fighters and bombers, and B-52 bomber aircraft for controlled release of ordnance on targets during periods of darkness or adverse weather.[47/] The most significant factors in achieving accuracy on COMBAT SKYSPOT missions were: (1) aircraft attitude at the bomb release point; (2) bomb dispersion; (3) turbulent air mass; (4) ground controller and pilot coordination; and (5) formation releases.[48/]

Data on the accuracy of COMBAT SKYSPOT missions were obtained from visual reconnaissance by FACs, photography, eye witnesses, and electronic measurement. Of these methods, the latter was most often used for accuracy scoring.[49/]

As of 1 November 1968, there were seven MSQ sites in operation. On 28 November 1968, OL-25 operation was discontinued to prepare equipment for movement to a new location at Mukdahan, Thailand. This relocation was needed to provide better coverage of the busy, South Laos interdiction area. The new site was scheduled to be operational by 31 December 1968.[50/]

An example of the Circular Error Average (CEA) reported for the seven MSQ sites is shown in Figure 7.[51/] A consideration which affected the accuracy of delivery was the lack of flexibility of the ordnance release pattern (coverage) on various type targets. The release (pickle) point

COMBAT SKYSPOT
TACTICAL AIRCRAFT STATISTICS

1-30 November 1968

MSQ SITE	MISSIONS	SORTIES	BOMBS	CEA*
Bien Hoa OL-21	137	247	1024	263 (feet)
Pleiku OL-22	222	436	2393	276
Nakhon Phanom OL-23	486	1262	8132	350
OL-27	467	1312	9332	320
Hue Phu Bai OL-24	413	765	4770	269
Quang Tri OL-25	136	283	1750	242
Binh Thuy OL-26	146	280	1250	390
	2007	4585	28651	312 (Avg)

* Electronic Measurement

FIGURE 7

was figured for the first bomb to hit the target; therefore, with the intervalometer settings on the MERs/TERs, the majority of the bombs were likely to cover only the last half of an area target such as a truck park. A technique used by some flight leaders was to vary the spacing of aircraft within the formation. Close formation was used for point targets, and a spread formation with about 50 feet between aircraft for area targets. However, a more effective coverage could probably have been attained, if calculations had been based on the middle bomb (rather than the first) hitting the target. Flight leaders also needed more flexibility in making decisions on timing/spacing of bomb release. Since MSQ-77 sites did not have target folders, they did not know the size of the area of a given target. The only target information they had was the Universal Transverse Mercator (UTM) coordinates and the target name.

With the exception of thunderstorms and turbulence, weather did not have a serious impact on the effectiveness of COMBAT SKYSPOT (CSS) missions. Nevertheless, problems which were either directly or indirectly attributable to weather/darkness were encountered in varying degrees by most SEA operational units utilizing MSQ-77 for ordnance delivery.

The relative inflexibility of run-in headings on COMBAT SKYSPOT mission resulted in two significant problems: (1) the MSQ Radar could not paint weather ahead of the attack aircraft. As a result, when thunderstorms were sighted, either visually or by airborne radar, the flight leader had to request a new run-in vector from the ground controller. If it were impossible (or time did not permit) to obtain a new vector, the flight was forced to break off the run; and (2) in more highly defended areas of North Vietnam or Laos, AAA was an ever-increasing threat to aircraft on CSS missions. Continually hitting the same target from the same direction, altitude, and often at the same time over target (TOT), gave the enemy gunners an unnecessary advantage. Since analysis of AAA reports had indicated a definite increase in the number of CSS flights being fired upon, any advantages afforded the enemy were viewed with concern. The lack of flexibility of CSS missions created an even greater danger when operations were conducted in the vicinity of a SAM ring or under IMC.[52]

The 8th TFW stressed the importance of conducting CSS missions only as required by weather conditions, which precluded visual strikes or when all other control agencies/strikes were saturated. The Wing also reasoned that night/strike/armed reconnaissance proficiency required continual practice to achieve maximum effectiveness and a heavy emphasis on CSS missions, when not required, negated valuable training and maintaining proficiency.[53]

To obtain an idea of just how much emphasis was being placed on CSS missions, and also to determine approximately how much of the total strike effort was devoted to nighttime operations, a computer run was made using random samples of data compiled for the period of 1 October 1967 through 11 January 1969. For the purpose of this study, total (USAF) strike

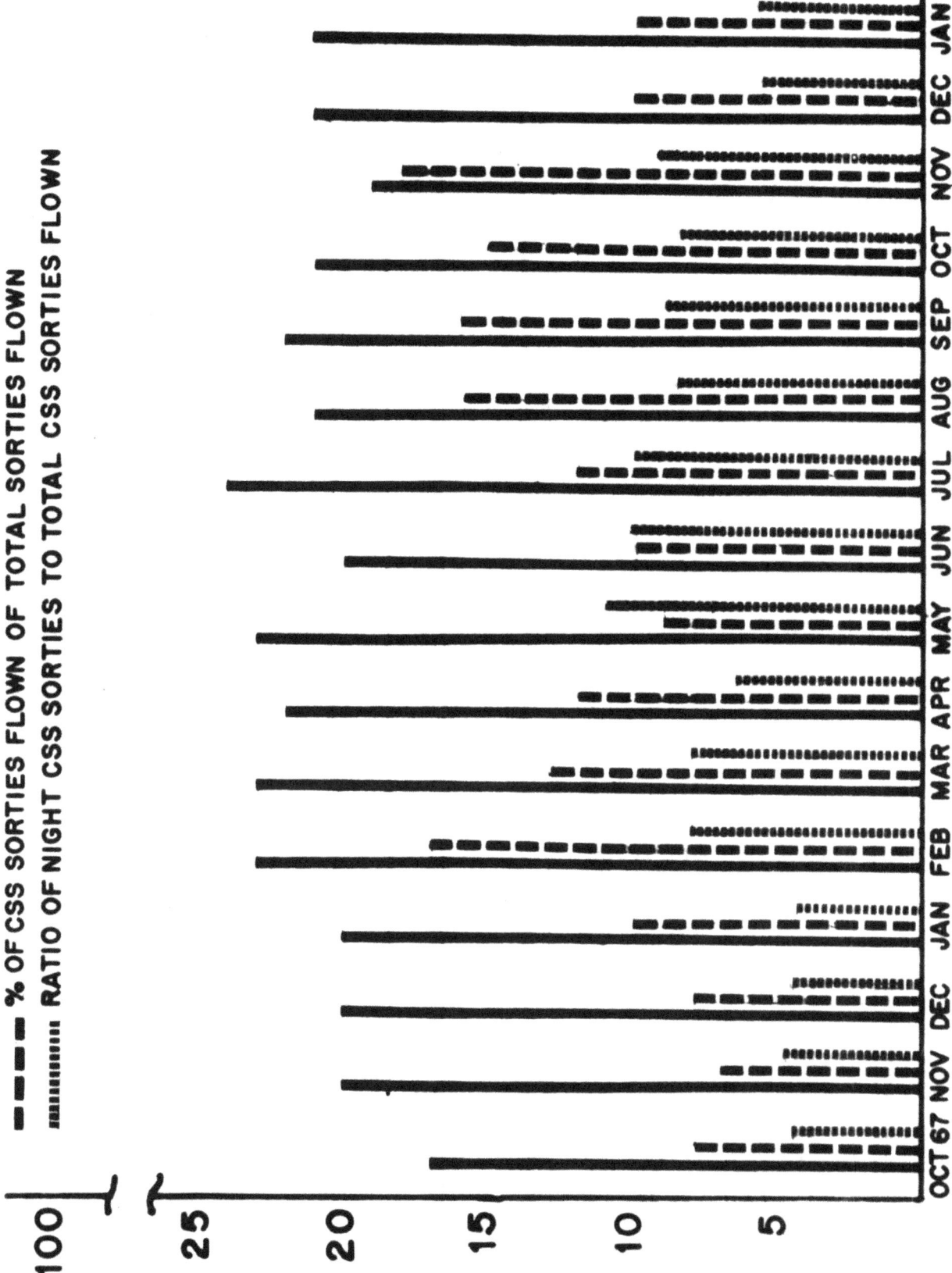

FIGURE 8

sorties included close air support, direct air support, interdiction and armed recon missions, flown in-country and out-country and during daylight and darkness. The results of this study are shown in Figure 8.[54/] For the month of October 1967, these results indicated that out of the total sorties flown, approximately 17 percent were flown at night, while eight percent of the total flown were COMBAT SKYSPOT sorties, both day and night. Of the total CSS sorties flown, approximately 57 percent (not to be read from the ordinate scale) were flown at night. The highest percentage (24 percent) of night sorties were flown in July 1968. During the same month, 12 percent of the total sorties flown were COMBAT SKYSPOT. Of the total CSS flown, approximately 76 percent were flown at night. Although the findings of this study could not be considered conclusive evidence, they did indicate that considerable emphasis was indeed being placed upon CSS missions.

The inflexibility of CSS missions was regarded as being too restrictive by the 35th TFW. Although CSS controllers had recently begun to provide GCI weather advisories during the final run-in, they were considered as being too general and not given until solicited by the crew. Since the MSQ Radar did not have a weather capability, the Wing was in favor of the CRC/GCI Center having a heading and distance to a clear weather area available during all CSS weather missions.[55/]

Carrying mixed ordnance loads, such as napalm externally and hard bombs internally, caused a unique problem for B-57s of the 8th TBS.

Since it was against the Seventh Air Force policy to use COMBAT SKYSPOT for mixed ordnance, two runs were required. Quite often the controlling agency directed the delivery of hard bombs, and then either sent the aircraft back to the base with the napalm, or turned the aircraft over to a FAC for a visual drop of the napalm. These restrictions sometimes compounded the fuel reserve problem.[56/]

As mentioned previously, the SST-181 (Music Box) transmitter greatly increased the effective range of the MSQ Radar. After installation in some of the F-100s assigned to the 37th TFW (installation was still underway in the remaining aircraft), the SST-181 greatly increased the effectiveness and reliability of the Wing's CSS missions.[57/] The lack of "Music Boxes" in some F-100s assigned to the 31st TFW caused numerous scheduling problems, and reduced flexibility in the diversion of aircraft to CSS missions when weather conditions precluded the visual delivery of ordnance. At the time (15 December 1968), only 60 percent of the Wing's F-100D aircraft were equipped with radar beacons. The two ANG squadrons assigned to the Wing, were equipped with F-100Cs; none of these aircraft had "Music Boxes" installed.[58/]

The 366th TFW experienced excessive holding delays due to saturation of CSS facilities. These delays frequently forced stike aircraft to return to the base unexpended. The lack of flexibility on the part of MSQ sites in using reciprocal run-in headings to the target was of major concern to the 366th TFW. On many occasions, the Wing found the distance en route to the IP had been increased by 75-100 miles to make use of a common IP when a run on the reciprocal heading would have been satisfactory. An additional benefit derived from the use of multiple IPs for a single target was a reduction in susceptibility of strike aircraft to defensive barrage antiaircraft fire.[59/]

Summary

In SEA, it was characteristic of the enemy to take advantage of darkness to resupply his forces and launch ground attacks on friendly forces. Accordingly, USAF was forced to expand its night operations to counter this tactic. The impact of darkness on these operations, although great, did not severely limit their effectiveness. If a target could be visually acquired, the probability of its destruction was increased.

Weather conditions such as thunderstorms caused deviations from run-in headings or mission abort, resulting in a serious impact on COMBAT SKYSPOT missions. Although a CSS mission could be flown in turbulence, accuracy of ordnance delivery was greatly reduced. The difficulties imposed by weather did not end with completion of ordnance delivery. COMBAT SKYSPOT missions, however, were not seriously impaired by darkness or non-turbulent weather.

CHAPTER V

IMPACT OF DARKNESS AND WEATHER ON
EGRESS AND RECOVERY

Egress from the target area and recovery at a designated airbase, were important phases of the mission profile. Flight join-up (when applicable) during egress from the target was complicated by conditions of darkness or weather. Normally, the flight leader would light the afterburner, turn on wing or refueling probe lights, or use similar means to affect join-up recognition.[1/] If available, airborne and ground radar were used to expedite join-up. When hostile ground fire was a factor, clouds made it easier for enemy gunners to acquire their target and using external or afterburner added to this hazard. The 35th TFW recommended that the UHF/DF modification be accelerated to simplify night/weather join-up.[2/]

Egress from the target area was highly critical in areas where MIGs were a threat. Loss of flight integrity jeopardized all members of the flight and a temporarily lost wingman was extremely vulnerable.[3/] Close formation enabled flight members to check each other's aircraft for battle damage or hung ordnance. If either condition existed, it was possible that a dangerous situation could develop, especially if fuel were a critical factor.[4/] An Aladdin-type hand-held light with a strong, focusable beam would have been an immense aid for determining post strike battle, damage, or hung ordnance.

Night operations in areas of heavy traffic increased the possibility of mid-air collision, especially when aircraft were operating blacked-out. Under these conditions, extreme caution was essential when egressing the target area.[5]

Under normal operating conditions, and discounting emergencies or other critical events, egress from the target was accomplished with minimum difficulty.

Recovery and Landing

Other than increasing the accident potential, darkness did not cause any significant problems during recovery and landing. During night recoveries, most operational units utilized IMC procedures, with aircraft making individual or two-ship approaches.[6] Darkness made it difficult to detect hung ordnance. If not detected, and approach and landing speeds were not adjusted, a hazardous situation was created. To minimize this danger, the 37th TFW thought pylon "station empty" indicator lights should have been installed.[7]

The possibility of the recovery base being attacked by enemy rockets was an important consideration. Diversion to an alternate base during night or marginal weather conditions could have caused serious problems due to low fuel reserves.[8] Weather seriously complicated the recovery process. The number of problems encountered were directly related to the navigational aids and terminal approach facilities available at the different air bases in SEA. In almost all recovery situations fuel was a critical factor. This was particularly true following a large strike when numerous aircraft were being recovered. Invariably during periods of bad weather conditions, approach facilities were saturated. Loss of radar contact with GCA aircraft was not uncommon. After landing, narrow, wet runways (like those at Ubon AB, Thailand) made directional control difficult and effective braking action nearly impossible.[9/]

Oversaturation of air operations at Da Nang AB, South Vietnam presented the problem of launching or recovering aircraft, while emergencies were in progress or weather conditions deteriorated. Tactical operations demanded priority handling, and were often extremely difficult to manage or supervise. Wet runway operations were very hazardous, and without dual runways would have been impossible.[10/] Both runways 17R and 35L had a U.S. Marine MOREST arresting system installed at the 6,000-foot point. However, when landing to the South, some F-4 aircraft skidded off the runway prior to reaching the MOREST. The 366th TFW thought that locating a MOREST at a point 3,000 feet from the approach end should minimize this problem.[11/]

The lack of grooved runways added considerably to the complications and consequently, increased landing risks during wet runway operations. Runway grooving would have provided the drainage necessary to counter hydroplaning, and would have diminished the grave risk involved when landing

F-4 aircraft on the narrow, high-crowned runways, often under crosswind conditions.[12/] Traffic Control Agencies required constant supervision and direction from the 366th TFW to insure their having tactical priorities. The effect of prior Air Route Traffic Control (ARTC)/International Civil Aviation Organization (ICAO) rules instilled in the thinking of many traffic controllers, required considerable reeducation and ultimately 7AF command assistance.[13/] In the interest of flying safety, the 31st TFW, operating out of Tuy Hoa, AB, conducted all night approaches and landings under IMC procedures. For actual runway touchdown, there were few visual references available to aid in depth perception. Under these conditions, instrument approaches decreased the possibility of landing accidents.[14/]

Recovery under unfavorable weather conditions presented some serious difficulties because of factors peculiar to Tuy Hoa AB. First, runway 03 had no published instrument approach, because of mountains located four miles from the approach end of the runway. Therefore, all instrument approaches were made to runway 21 with a circling approach to runway 03. Under rain or low visibility conditions, this approach was hazardous for high performance jet aircraft. In addition, there were delays due to departures on runway 03 and approaches to runway 21. Further complicating the situation was the tendency of the Radar Approach Control Center (RAPCON) to lose radar contact with aircraft when rain showers were prevalent, plus the inadequate windshield rain-removal system of F-100s.[15/]

Night and unfavorable flying weather recoveries at Phan Rang AB caused some unique problems for the 35th TFW. Phan Rang was surrounded on three sides by mountainous terrain. The TACAN approach in use on 15 December 1968 required the pilot to fly an arc approach that placed the aircraft in close proximity to high terrain. However, another TACAN approach, providing a straight-in approach was in the process of being implemented. At the time, Phan Rang did not have an operational GCA. 16/

The 18th TBS considered inadequate fuel reserve to be a potential problem during weather recoveries. Since the B-57 did not have an inflight refueling capability, this problem was minimized through careful supervision and aircrew discipline as regarded minimum fuel requirements. 17/

The 355th TFW was also concerned about the additional fuel required for ICM recoveries. In a force-size recovery, the flow of traffic could have easily saturated the control and GCA radars. To preclude this possibility, the Wing's aircraft recovered in two-ship flights and individual flights remained with the post-strike tanker, until an orderly flow of traffic was achieved. 18/

Summary

Under normal operating conditions, and discounting emergencies or other critical events, egress from target under night or unfavorable flying weather conditions was accomplished with minimum difficulty. The egress join-up was complicated in the same manner as takeoff join-up, the same problems and solutions were applicable. The necessity for re-join evolved from the requirement for maintaining flight integrity, expediting recoveries, and checking aircraft for battle damage or hung ordnance.

Although darkness was of no great consequence during the recovery phase, it did increase the accident potential during approach and landing. On the other hand, weather conditions imposed serious problems and constraints on the recovery process. Factors such as battle damage, hung ordnance, low fuel reserve, and emergencies contributed further complications to the recovery phase. During inclement weather, traffic control facilities at most bases became saturated and loss of radar contact with GCA aircraft was not uncommon. Narrow, ungrooved runways greatly increased the landing risks during periods of rainy weather and made arresting barriers absolutely necessary. Coupled with the lack of GCA and ILS equipment at some bases, all of these factors made the recovery and landing process an extremely critical phase of the mission profile.

CHAPTER VI

IMPACT OF DARKNESS AND WEATHER ON AC-47 GUNSHIP OPERATIONS

The AC-47 arrived in SEA in November 1965 at Tan Son Nhut AB, South Vietnam. Initially, there were 20 aircraft assigned to the 4th Air Commando Squadron (ACS); later the 3d ACS was organized and each squadron was assigned 16 aircraft. Late in 1968, the ACS designation was changed to Special Operations Squadron. The first gunship operations were flown at night, but during January 1966, daylight interdiction missions were conducted in Laos. By June 1966, four aircraft had been lost to enemy ground fire and daylight operations were discontinued. Subsequently, AC-47 (Spooky) operations were restricted to night operations. Normally, Spooky operations were confined to in-country; occasionally, however, the aircraft were diverted into Laos and the DMZ.[1]

Background

The AC-47 fixed-wing gunship was primarily employed at night in support of US/Free World Military Forces (US/FWMF). It proved to be an outstanding defensive weapons system, which had the capabilities of staging on target for an extended period of time, maintaining a sustained and accurate fire on hostile targets, and providing its own target illumination. During the early period of AC-47 operations in SEA, exploitation of its offensive fire capability was attempted during daylight hours. These operations resulted in four aircraft being lost to enemy ground fire within a period of about three months. The low operating altitudes (the first AC-47 to be shot down by enemy ground fire was hit at 1,000 feet AGL), and slow airspeed of the aircraft made it extremely vulnerable to ground fire in a hostile environment. Consequently, Spooky operations were restricted to night operations. Whether daylight operations conducted at altitudes above the envelope of small arms fire would prove feasible, remained to be seen. As it turned out, Spooky operations were forced into the hours of darkness and resulted in a trade off of ammunition for illumination devices. It also proved to be one of the most effective night defensive weapon systems in SEA.

The primary mission of the 14th Special Operations Wing's (SOW) AC-47 gunships was to defend installations, strategic hamlets, and fortresses against hostile attacks, and supplement strike aircraft in defense of Free World Military Forces. Gunships were armed with 7.62-mm miniguns. When fired from 3,000 feet AGL, these guns had limited effectiveness against well-protected troops, but the effect against troops in the open was devastating. Knowledge of this fact often caused the enemy to discontinue his attack when Spooky aircraft were in the immediate area. Additional utilization combined the flares of the gunship with ordnance of fighter aircraft under the control of a FAC. Primary utilization of Spooky aircraft was on Combat Air Patrol in a designated area to conduct visual, airborne surveillance of possible rocket/mortar launch sites, and to act as an airborne alert for dispatch to targets in minimum time. 2/

Problems and Limitations Attributed to Darkness

Since the AC-47 mission was oriented to night operations, darkness had a minimal effect on its overall operation. En route to the target area, navigation was accomplished with TACAN, Radio Compass, and GCI. At low altitude and long ranges, TACAN was unreliable and Radio Compass did not provide an accurate means of navigation to isolated target areas. Normally, the highest possible en route altitude was maintained to take advantage of improved TACAN reception and GCI coverage. With few exceptions, darkness had little effect on the en route portion of the mission profile. [3]

Neither did darkness have any serious impact on target acquisition, if some type of ground reference light was available. In isolated areas where there were absolutely no visible ground lights, target acquisition was much more difficult. In these areas, a light presented by the ground controller was almost essential. In the event a light could not be displayed for fear of disclosing friendly positions, it was possible for the ground controller to literally talk the pilot onto the target by directing the gunship in relation to terrain features. Frequently, friendly ground personnel did not have adequate means (strobe lights, tracer ammunition, flashlights, white phosphorous, fire arrows, etc.) for marking their positions. Flare illumination was not always feasible, if friendly forces did not want to disclose their position to the enemy. What was needed, according to the 14th SOW, was a standard means of marking friendly ground positions. For example, a system whereby the aircrew could utilize an IR sensor or Starlight Scope to locate a pinpoint position or reference signal on the ground, would have been an invaluable aid in locating friendly positions without exposing them to the enemy. [4]

Problems and Limitations Attributable to Weather

The impact of weather conditions on Spooky operations ranged from minimal to mission abort, and was dependent upon the type and severity of the weather. Few missions were sufficiently critical to justify ordering a crew to a target, which would require penetrating areas of severe or extreme turbulence. Aside from the danger to the aircraft structure, turbulence in the target area made it extremely difficult to accurately deliver ordnance. 5/

Clouds, as a restriction to visibility, had no adverse effects on ingressing or egressing the target area, except for clearance related to terrain and other aircraft. Within the target area, low clouds interfered with target acquisition, and if the target could not be visually acquired, supporting fire could not be provided. Due to cloud coverage, flares were sometimes dropped in the general target area by using a TACAN/DME fix, but accuracy was significantly reduced. The adverse effect of clouds on flare coverage was reduced by expending multiple flares on each pass, but of course this tactic reduced the period of illumination available for each target. The effects of clouds as a restriction to visibility could be reduced, if the base of the clouds were high enough to permit maneuvering underneath. The lowest practical altitude for gunship operation was 2,500 feet AGL. Below this altitude, the aircraft entered the small arms fire envelope and flares would still be burning as they hit the ground, depriving the aircrew of its full capability to light up the area. Also, when flares were dropped beneath an overcast, the aircraft was silhouetted against the clouds and increased its vulnerability to ground fire.[6]

High winds created problems which had a deteriorating effect on gunship operations. For ordnance delivery, a maximum expending firing circle was difficult to maintain when large wind corrections were necessary. Since the gunsight did not have a wind compensation capability, high winds required the use of "Kentucky windage" when sighting and firing. Using this method, accuracy was somewhat reduced.[7]

Spooky gunships did not have the capability of delivering ordnance through an overcast. Although accuracy could not be assured, flares could be deployed through an overcast into the general target area by using a TACAN Radial/DME fix. Tests were conducted to determine the feasibility of using the COMBAT SKYSPOT capability during weather operations. Both illumination and ground marker flares were dropped under COMBAT SKYSPOT control. The accuracy achieved in placing ground markers was encouraging; however, the low operating altitude of the AC-47 made radar skin paint difficult and restricted the usable range of CSS equipment. Range would have been increased considerably had the SST-181 X-Band Beacon been installed. In addition, clouds with significant moisture had an adverse effect on radar lock-on capability. Tests were also conducted to evaluate the capability of CSS to vector the aircraft to the target and maintain it in a firing orbit. Again, radar range was a limiting factor and accuracy of about 300 meters was the best attained. This was not acceptable for utilization at that time.[8/]

Conclusions

The AC-47 proved to be an extremely capable and effective weapon system for night operations and had the capability of staying on target for an extended period of time, maintaining a sustained and accurate fire on hostile targets, and providing its own illumination. Daylight exploitation of its offensive firepower capability, while operating within the small arms ground fire envelope of a hostile environment, however, resulted in unacceptable losses. Subsequently, the AC-47 was restricted to night operations. As a result, illumination flares were required, and caused a reduction in the amount of ammunition which could be carried. In addition, darkness created problems in the target acquisition process, particularly in isolated areas where there were no visible ground lights. In these areas, a marker light presented by the ground controller was almost essential for acquiring the target.

The impact of weather on Spooky operations ranged from minimal to mission abort. Few missions were sufficiently critical to justify penetrating heavy or severe turbulence. Aside from the danger to aircraft structure, turbulence or high winds in the target area made accurate ordnance delivery extremely difficult. When the target could not be visually acquired due to low visibilities, supporting fire could not be delivered.

Ordnance could not be delivered through an overcast. Although illumination and ground markers could be delivered utilizing TACAN/DME fix, or COMBAT SKYSPOT, accuracy could not be guaranteed.

Lessons Learned

The most significant lessons learned were:

During daylight conditions in a hostile environment, the AC-47 was highly vulnerable to enemy ground fire, if operations were conducted at altitudes which placed the aircraft within the range of small arms weapons. Restricting altitudes to a minimum of 3,500 feet AGL in a permissive environment (no small arms larger than .50 calibre), should permit daylight operations to be conducted with an acceptable risk.

In isolated operating areas where navigational aids were unreliable or nonexistent, pinpoint target acquisition and maintaining terrain clearance were limiting factors in accomplishing the mission.

The 7.62-mm miniguns employed on AC-47 gunships had limited effectiveness against well-protected troops, but were devastating against troops in the open.

For night/weather operations, the effectiveness, reliability, and adaptability of the AC-47 and future gunships would be increased by the following:

.Increasing TACAN and radar coverage by the installation of additional or remote sites.

.Increase area of radio voice coverage by installation of remote transmit/receive sites.

.Installation of Selective Identification Feature equipment on each gunship to facilitate rapid and positive radar control.

.Installation of SST-181 X-Band Beacons on each aircraft to increase capabilities of MSQ-77 to direct accurate ordnance delivery periods of inclement weather.

.Development of an identification system whereby gunships could pinpoint targets or friendly force positions.

.Development of an air-launched flare with longer burn capability.

CHAPTER VII

IMPACT OF DARKNESS AND WEATHER
ON AIRLIFT AND DEFOLIATION OPERATIONS

The mission of the 834th Air Division (AD) was the management and control of the in-country Tactical Airlift operations. To perform this mission, the 834th AD utilized C-130s from the 315th AD, C-123s from the 315th Special Operations Wing, and C-7As from the 483d Tactical Airlift Wing. The outstanding accomplishments of the airlift mission in SEA have been duly recorded. Even so, as will be seen in the following discussion, darkness and weather conditions had a serious impact on airlift and defoliation operations.

Airlift, Airland Operations

Darkness imposed several limitations on C-130 aircraft from the 315th Air Division. These limitations were primarily due to the limited number of in-country airfields that were night-capable. Of the 77 airfields in Vietnam that were suitable for C-130 operations, only 17 were equipped and able to support night operations on a routine basis. Of the remaining 60 airfields, the majority were classified as Type I or II airfields. (Appendix II.) A number of factors were responsible for this limitation and included: lack of runway and taxiway lights; unmarked or hazardous obstructions on, or in the vicinity of the airfield; and lack of airfield security from enemy attack (the latter factor was the prime restriction for C-7A and C-123 night operations). Further restrictions of this nature included the fact that users often could not get to an airfield in the early morning because of a lack of secure access roads. Therefore, airlanded loads had to arrive sufficiently early in the afternoon to permit the user to claim his cargo and truck it to his base of operations prior to nightfall, at which time, the surface access routes again became insecure. The result of this restriction was that such airfields were not only a limiting factor during actual hours of darkness, but also lift time in and out of these airfields was lost. This daily loss amounted to two or more hours--one hour after first light and one hour prior to nightfall.[1/]

In addition, the limited number of airfields routinely available for night operations restricted the total amount of cargo that was accessible to the cargo fleet. Generally, the major aerial ports were the only ones which generated sufficient cargo to warrant continuous operations. Many of the destinations for the cargo, however, were unable to accept aircraft at night; thus an effective shipping embargo of approximately 12 hours per day was levied on much of the available cargo at the major ports.[2/]

Many airfields used by the C-130s had night and all-weather capabilities. Although C-7s and C-123s could have operated out of those bases, the fact that these bases were C-130-capable dictated scheduling the higher cargo load capability of the C-130, particularly between major ports.[3/]

The mission of the 483d Tactical Airlift Wing (TAW) was that of providing intra-theater airlift in support of military forces, civic actions, and the Agency for International Development (AID).4/ Equipped with C-7A aircraft, the Wing operated within the various Field Force areas of operations down to the smallest combat unit. Characteristic of this operation were extremely austere landing strips (many of which were barely recognizable as airstrips), where navigational aids were either limited or nonexistent. For this reason, the C-7A operation was almost exclusively a tactical VMC operation and limited, when low-ceiling visibilities prevailed, to those airfields having tactical VMC minimum conditions. In Vietnam, fortunately, this condition rarely persisted or prevailed throughout the entire country.5/

The 483d TAW flew approximately 15,000 sorties per month, of which more than 50 percent were flown into forward airfields where there were no approach facilities and lighting varied from nonexistent to sand-filled flare pots. Those operations were severely hampered by darkness and weather conditions, and therefore in normal day-to-day operations, the Wing's airlift mission began at first light and ended at dusk. In marginal weather conditions, the priority of the mission determined whether a landing would be attempted.6/

Of major concern to the 483d TAW was weather encountered en route to the destination. When weather made it impossible to maintain VMC, the pilot was forced to either fly in the weather (condition "popeye"), or abort the mission. Operating in "popeye" conditions was essentially IMC, and the area radar sites provided horizontal clearance from other aircraft; however, they were unable to guarantee vertical separation. If the area radar sites could have provided positive control, most missions into airfields with instrument approach facilities could have been safely and successfully completed. 7/

The mission of the 315th Special Operations Wing (SOW) was to accomplish airlift operations as directed by the Commander, 834th Air Division, and defoliation tasks under the direction of the Commander, Seventh Air Force. Assigned aircraft were C-123B/K and UC-123B/K. 8/

The 315th SOW was required, at one time, to fly a night airlift line. This mission was normally fragged into Type III (fully operational) airfields such as Tan Son Nhut, Bien Hoa, Binh Thuy, Pleiku, Tuy Hoa, and Cam Ranh Bay. The crew duty time on these missions was ten and a half hours and one crew was normally scheduled for two consecutive nights. However, the missions were not productive and the flying hours frequently exceeded the tonnage carried. 9/

The C-123 had the same limitations insofar as operations into VMC, daylight-only airfields were concerned. Those small, isolated airfields, having no facilities for navigation or instrument approaches, were used daily by C-123s so long as the weather remained at or above Tactical

VMC minimums. The C-123 had a further limitation in that its crosswind capability was restricted by its narrow main tread.[10/] During inclement weather, many of the forward strips became too slippery for safe operations even during daylight hours. In many instances, the rough terrain surrounding the objective zone prohibited a letdown at night or in weather, except by very accurate approach systems which could provide both azimuth and glide slope information.

At many of the forward bases, the normal letdown procedure was to "find a hole" in the clouds or overcast and proceed by pilotage to the destination. Of course, this procedure was not always possible and many missions were aborted. Often, missions could not be completed even with 1,000 to 1,500-foot ceilings, due to the hazards of enemy ground fire and artillery. Egress from a landing (or drop zone) during night or weather conditions, required that the pilot have detailed knowledge of the surrounding terrain. In addition, sufficient altitude had to be attained before communications and radar contact could be established with controlling agencies for entry back into the air traffic control system.[11/]

During unfavorable flying weather conditions, the 315th SOW found that excessive traffic, particularly at the main terminal bases such as Saigon, Bien Hoa, and Cam Ranh Bay, caused several problems. According to the 315th SOW, the traffic control capability in these areas became saturated very quickly during periods of inclement weather and resulted in long delays in arrivals and departures. On some occasions, it was impossible to depart from Phan Rang on an instrument flight plan because the Saigon Center would not (or could not) issue a clearance without extensive delay. The lack of radar at Phan Rang also complicated traffic control procedures.[12/]

Most of the 315th SOW's airlift operations during IMC were conducted on tactical clearances and relied upon Control and Reporting Center (CRC) facilities and hemispheric quadrantal separation for traffic avoidance. On numerous occasions, while under radar monitorship of CRC, traffic was observed in close proximity, but was not reported by the CRC agency. Incidents such as this tended to make the Wing's aircrews extremely reluctant to fly in actual instrument conditions, because they could not be guaranteed adequate separation or traffic advisories. Further complicating the air traffic control system was the mixture of tactical traffic operating under military regulations and international traffic operating under International Civil Aviation Organization rules. During periods of inclement weather, the frustrations created by excessive ground times and traffic congestion, coupled with hazardous flying conditions, greatly contributed to aircrew fatigue.[13/]

Airdrop and Extraction Operations

The 834th Air Division Tactical Airlift aircraft had the capability to effectively conduct airdrop operations during periods of darkness. Except for emergency airdrop of ammunition to Special Forces Camps by C-7As, this darkness capability was not used due to the inability of the user to provide a secure Drop Zone (DZ). With one notable exception (the resupply of Khe Sanh), weather did have a restrictive impact on airdrop operations in SEA. Low ceilings and visibilities delayed or prevented delivery of supplies by airdrop or extractions. Delays and rescheduling of airdrop/extraction operations also occurred in high-threat areas, where satisfactory ceilings prevailed for airdrop/extraction operations, but the ceilings were too low to permit required fighter support. When available, Army gunships were used in high-threat areas to support airdrop/extraction operations when ceilings prevented fighter operations. During the resupply of Khe Sanh (21 Jan thru 8 Apr 1968), the 834th Air Division developed a procedure which permitted continued airdrop of supplies under IMC conditions. The procedure consisted of a letdown to drop altitude under GVA on an inbound heading to the DZ. This was followed by a "mark" over a specific geographical point given by either GCA or Marine radar (TPQ-10). From the "mark", Doppler and stopwatch were used to place the aircraft at the computed air release point (CARP) over the DZ. There were 138 (38 percent) of the Container Delivery System (CDS) drops at Khe Sanh under IMC conditions with an average circular error of 133 yards. [14/]

Airlift Combat Operations

During the latter part of January 1968, there was much concern that the proposed truce during the Vietnamese holiday, "Tet", would not be honored by the Viet Cong. This concern was well-founded since, on

29 January 1968, a combined enemy force composed of hardcore Viet Cong units and North Vietnamese Regulars launched what has been defined as the "biggest offensive of the war". At the outset of this offensive, highly concentrated attacks were made on Ban Me Thuot City and the small garrison there. Units of the 315th SOW were called upon to fly reinforcements from the 23d Ranger Battalion, based at Bao Loc, into Ban Me Thuot City. Although the weather and lighting were marginal at both fields, the troop movement and airlift of associated equipment and supplies were accomplished with the Ban Me Thuot airfield illuminated only with vehicle headlights. Fifty-four sorties, flown through adverse night weather and ground fire, enabled the defenders to secure the base. 15/

On 2 February 1968, Vinh Long City and its Special Forces Camp were under intense hostile fire. Large sections of the city were in flames and under direct enemy control. Control of the airfield varied between the defenders and the large, heavily armed enemy force. The defenders were able to hold consistently only the northeast area (compound) of the airfield. With munitions and rations running low, a C-123 was configured to provide an Emergency Resupply airdrop of 10,000 pounds of munitions and supplies. While the aircraft was en route to Vinh Long, the defenders gained control of the airfield and a decision was made to airland the supplies. A maximum performance assault landing was initiated for the blacked out airfield with AC-47s and Huey gunships providing fire suppression gunfire. The landing, offload, and take off were accomplished in approximately five minutes with field illumination provided by an airdropped flare. 16/

During the same period, another tactical emergency resupply airdrop was required at Kontum City. Again, most of the city and the airfield were in flames and under enemy control. The defenders were confined to the small compound on the northwest edge of town. The compound, totally blacked out, was located with the use of short duration white phosphorous grenades while the drop aircraft circled the 75-by 150-yard compound. The drop was made by using the surrounding fires and illuminated areas as checkpoints. All five bundles, 10,000 pounds of high explosive ammunition, were delivered on target. This was the first low-level night airdrop mission made by the 315th SOW. 17/

During and subsequent to this period, the 315th SOW aircraft flew numerous Tactical Emergency Resupply missions in support of the Marine forces at Khe Sanh. Totally outnumbered and surrounded, the Marines had to rely on air delivery for resupply and evacuation of casualties and non-combatants. The C-123s were tasked to deliver the supplies which could not be airdropped. Visibility at Khe Sanh was frequently totally obscured and the ceiling was seldom more than 500 feet above the ground. Approaches were made using GCA, when the ceiling would not permit an assault approach. The C-123 performance data at Khe Sanh list 36 sorties, 43.3 tons airdropped and 765 troops airlanded. 18/

As a result of the difficulties encountered in providing air resupply to bases under attack, a "Khe Sanh" checklist was developed to counteract the impact of darkness and weather hazards. This checklist included the initial outbound route and altitude, and a checkpoint where a TAC IFR flight plan was to be initiated with a GCA or TACAN approach to Khe Sanh. An abbreviated turnaround checklist covered offload, onload, and configuration for take off. The route for return to the support base was also included.[19]

Unfavorable weather conditions, and particularly low ceilings, had a detrimental effect on the safety of landing aircraft. Low ceilings meant that the landing aircraft did not have the advantage of fighter support for suppressing ground fire and further, were forced to remain aligned with the GCA azimuth and glide slope until sighting the landing runway. This permitted the enemy to concentrate his attention and gunfire on the last portion of the GCA. With higher ceilings, fighter ground fire suppression was available and random, maximum performance assault landings were used to minimize the effect of hostile ground fire. Fighters were also used against the enemy artillery to permit the C-123 to land, offload and take off with a minimum chance of being disabled by the enemy artillery and mortars. In spite of these tactics, three C-123s were destroyed during the battle for Khe Sanh.[20]

Equipment Requirements

Since the beginning of the airlift mission in Vietnam, cargo delivery by aircraft has been hampered by inadequate navigational aids and terminal approach facilities. It was evident that to satisfy user needs, a highly mobile family of navigational and terminal approach aids would require development. As specific requirements could be defined, projects were initiated through the Southeast Asia Operational Requirements (SEAOR) process as specified by AFR 57-1 and included the following:[21/]

Portable Lighting. During the latter part of February 1966, SEAOR-40 (FY-66) was submitted for a portable lighting system, which would provide adequate night lighting at austere airfields in Vietnam. The need for mobile airfield lighting was well established. The airlift mission in Southeast Asia frequently required aircraft to operate from remote, poorly equipped, backwoods airstrips, which were not conducive to the installation and maintenance of a permanent lighting system. Night operations on these secondary airfields had been accomplished through use of primitive marking devices such as flare pots and cans of fuel-soaked sand. There was no visual aid which could provide aircrews with a visual landing glide slope reference. Such poor lighting devices were not only difficult to transport and set up, but added appreciably to the already hazardous missions of night time airlift. In addition, the lack of a satisfactory mobile lighting system also prevented the use of more than 30 percent of available airfields during the hours of darkness. The SEAOR-40 (FY-66) specified a portable design which would satisfy the following criteria:[22/]

> A Night Visual Illuminated Guidance System beacon which would provide long-range (8-NM) acquisition, positive LZ/DZ identification, accurate night drop release indication, and approach glide slope presentation.

- High intensity directional runway corner marker lights. These lights were to be green on the approach end of the runway and red at the terminal point.

- Omni-directional runway marker lights sufficient to outline a 3,000-foot airstrip. When used with 115V AC power these lights would have a single point, turn on/off capability.

- In addition this equipment listed, the Combat Control Team required a number of lightweight, battery-operated Strobe lights which could be utilized to aid in airfield acquisition or runway threshold definition.

IMC Airdrop. To provide an improved instrument airdrop capability SEAOR-67 (FY-67) was submitted in January 1967. At the time of submission of this SEAOR, a very limited, adverse weather capability existed through utilization of a ground radar station, which could direct aircraft to a release point (CARP). This system utilized a Marinet TPQ-10 radar complex. Using this system, however, required drop altitudes of 5,400 to 7,500 feet AGL, due to radar line of sight limitations. This caused drop circular error ranges of up to 600 meters, which in most situations was unsatisfactory due to the difficulty of recovering supplies in hostile areas. SEAOR-67 proposed the use of steerable parachutes with the TPQ-10 radar to achieve circular errors of 200 feet or less from a maximum drop altitude of 10,000 feet. Due to inadequate Air Force FY-68-69 funding, progress on this SEAOR could only be achieved through a joint 7AF/USARV program. At this date, such a program had not materialized; however, other methods of IMC airdrops were being studied. Details were not available but airdrop techniques, involving the use of portable TACAN or Instrument Landing System (ILS) equipment, were being considered.[23]

Portable ILS. In March of 1967 SEAOR-67 (FY-67) was submitted which established a requirement for a lightweight, man-portable, all-weather precision terminal approach capability. A system known as TALAR IV was being developed; it would weigh approximately 50 pounds and could be set up in 15 minutes. TALAR IV would provide a reliable precision approach capability for weather minimums of 200-foot ceiling and one-mile visibility. The ground equipment would consist of a microwave guidance system, which would provide precision glide stop and localizer information to aircraft equipped with a standard instrument landing system (ILS) cross pointer indicator. To utilize the TALAR IV system, aircraft would require minor modification to existing aircraft equipment and the installation of several black boxes. It was believed this system could more than double the number of airfields in Vietnam, which could be used by C-130 aircraft during inclement weather. Of the 175 airstrips in South Vietnam, only 22 had terminal landing aids. With the TALAR IV, an all-weather, precision approach capability could be provided to the remaining 153 airstrips at a nominal cost. Program schedules indicate the system should be operational by July 1969. [24/]

Portable GCA. To further extend the weather capability of the USAF airlift fleet, the requirement for a portable GCA system existed. This facility would by no means be as mobile as the TALAR IV (ILS), as it was expected to weigh in excess of 4,000 pounds, but it was considered portable, in that it would be transportable by C-7A aircraft. Furthermore, it would require approximately six hours to set up for operation. A prime requirement for this equipment was to provide control and surveillance of air traffic in the vicinity of an operating location during an airlift operation. In addition to its prime capability, the portable GCA unit could provide a valuable back-up for the TALAR IV precision approach equipment.[25/]

Portable TACAN. To provide an additional instrument navigational aid and approach capability to austere airfields or drop zones, a portable TACAN system was being developed under SEAOR-119 (FY-67). This SEAOR was submitted in April 1967 and identified the need for a system, which would facilitate the performance of high altitude jet and low altitude conventional approaches. Like the TALAR IV, the portable TACAN was to be designed for operation by Combat Control Team personnel. This system was to be designed in three configurations. The minimum capability, with a weight of 200 pounds, would provide UHF direction information only; a second configuration, weighing 400 pounds, would provide a single transmitter for direction and distance measuring; a third configuration, weighing 600 pounds would provide a back-up set with quick changeover, in case of failure of the primary. The simultaneous distance-measuring capability was expected to accommodate 50 aircraft. Since all C-130 aircraft were restricted from the use of TACAN as an approach aid due to aircraft equipment installation problems, SEAOR-84 (FY-67) was initiated to modify these aircraft. First delivery of the "lightweight" TACAN was scheduled for 1 August 1969.[26/]

All of the most urgent requirements were submitted as SEAOR, and when these navigational aids (NAVAIDS) became available, the 834th AD believed that complete all weather/night airlift operation would depend upon only the security of the airfield.[27/]

Defoliation Operations

Defoliation operations conducted by the 315th SOW were limited to daylight hours, with temperatures of less than 85 degrees, and winds not over ten knots per hour. Initial time on target was scheduled after sunrise and the only night operations were those involved in take off, assembly, and en route to the target area. The serious impact which unfavorable flying weather had on defoliation operations was well illustrated by the fact that the percentage of defoliation sorties lost due to weather varied from 12 percent in the best weather month, to 52 percent in the worst weather month. Ceiling and visibility minimums established for target areas over mountainous terrain were 500 feet and 5 miles. For nonmountainous terrain, these minimums were set at 300 feet and 3 miles. Fog in the target area caused the mission to be canceled, unless the fog was less than 100 feet thick and the target area could be accurately identified. The success of the defoliation mission was highly dependent upon the availability of fighters to escort and provide ground fire suppression for the spray aircraft. The ceiling requirements for fighter aircraft were determined by the tactics they used to deliver ordnance. Generally, these ceilings varied from 1,000 to 1,500 feet. Spray aircraft crews depended upon the FAC, who flew over the target area prior to their arrival, for their most reliable weather information.[28/]

Conclusions

These conclusions were drawn from past experience of airlift and defoliation operations conducted in SEA:

As of December 1968, only a limited all-weather airlift capability existed in SEA. In conditions of severe weather, airlift operations were restricted to those airfields equipped with the necessary navigational aids and approach and landing facilities. Of the 77 airfields in Vietnam which were suitable for C-130 operations, only 17 were so equipped and able to support weather/night operations on a routine basis.

The limited number of airfields routinely available for night operation restricted the total amount of cargo accessible to the airlift fleet. The major aerial ports, in general, were the only ones generating sufficient cargo to warrant continuous operation. However, many of the destinations for that cargo were unable to accept aircraft at night; thus, an effective shipping embargo for approximately 12 hours a day was levied on much of the cargo available in the major ports.

For the most part, the day-only airfields in use at the time (15 Dec 68) were very definitely dependent upon continued fair weather to render them suitable for sustained use. On many of these, the landing surface was such that, if wet, it was necessary for aircraft to reduce their cabin loads to assure a safe landing.

Limited capabilities of the air traffic control system did not permit expeditious handling of IMC traffic; thereby encouraging aircrews to attempt to fly under VMC during actual weather conditions. In addition, inadequate and unreliable letdown facilities at forward airstrips made it necessary for aircrews to make letdowns based upon their knowledge of the surrounding terrain features. A real danger lay in the possible overdependence on that knowledge.

Airlift effectiveness would have been improved had the capability of terminal radar at major supply bases been increased. Included in this capability was the requirement to accept and control traffic on short notice and the preclusion of the necessity for filing an IMC clearance on tactical sorties. Also needed, was a high volume, dependable radar flight following capability for all areas to include adequate coverage at low altitudes, terrain mapping and height finding equipment.

A method was needed for electronically determining an exact location with respect to ground personnel for accomplishing optimum airdrops to inaccessible areas during night/weather conditions. In addition, a visual display was needed to indicate the exact position and provide accurate wind drift corrections.

Defoliation missions were limited to daylight hours, due to the low level (100 feet above tree tops) altitude requirement for spray dispersal. Unfavorable flying weather caused the cancellation of a large percentage of defoliation missions; from 12 percent in the best weather month to 52 percent in the worst weather month.

Lessons Learned

The most significant lesson learned was to avoid the necessity of night/weather airlift operations into forward air bases. This could generally be done by maintaining a sufficient level of supplies at these bases, precluding the necessity of making delivery during conditions of night/weather or enemy activity. Unfavorable weather, which was normally encountered during a day's airlift operation, was to be avoided even if it meant flying above 10,000 feet for short periods of time. When weather could not be avoided, reliance was placed upon area radar for flight monitoring (this capability was not used extensively due to its limited capability to handle a large volume of traffic). Weather could also deny access to the forward operating bases by forcing the aircraft down into areas of heavy hostile ground fire, particularly if fighter support was not available.

Operations conducted during darkness and adverse weather conditions emphasized the need for equipment which would enable aircraft to make random directional approaches to combat drop areas, improve navigation capabilities and provide a system for precisely identifying the drop/release point. In addition, it was learned from actual experience that a mobile, terminal precision approach facility was an absolute necessity.

CHAPTER VIII
CONCLUSIONS

The force of the impact which darkness and unfavorable weather conditions exerted on USAF air operations in SEA was directly proportional to the severity of these two conditions when applied against a particular mission. During periods of darkness, certain missions such as: Psychological Warfare, Search and Rescue, Defoliation, and some portions of Airlift, could not be performed with an acceptable degree of safety and effectiveness. For other missions, darkness imposed undesirable limitations and restrictions, which seriously degraded mission effectiveness. Also, it was instrumental in determining selection of ordnance and tactics to be employed, seriously complicating all phases of the mission profile and creating an environment conducive to vertigo and spatial disorientation.

Weather was the single, most important factor which determined that a mission could be successfully accomplished. Depending upon its severity, weather either decreased mission effectiveness, caused target diversions, necessitated the use of alternate means of ordnance (pay load) delivery or forced complete cancellation of the mission. In view of the inadequate night/weather capability of possessed equipment, aircrews achieved remarkable success throughout SEA in the accomplishment of their respective mission.

Some of the most important conclusions concerning the impact of darkness/weather on air operations in SEA include the following:

There was no aircraft-contained, instrument weather target acquisition and bombing system capability available for use in SEA. The only back-up capability available when weather precluded visual deliveries was radar bombing utilizing COMBAT SKYSPOT or the Marine radar bombing system, TPQ-10. These systems provided low-level accuracy, which was useful for harassment, but not accurate enough to be used near friendly troops. With the equipment available, 7AF had difficulty in supporting troops in contact when ceilings were 300 feet and visibilities were two miles or less. (There were very few documented instances where close air support was performed during such poor weather conditions.) Sensor equipped aircraft such as the AC-130 and AC-119K, should improve this support capability, if the field forces are equipped with reflective panels, portable radar beacons, or other marking capability.[1]

Improvement in techniques and equipment was required for detection and target acquisition of trucks concealed in shadows and under heavy vegetation, for targets in very low levels of light, and in conditions of poor visibility or weather.[2]

Continued development was needed for long duration, night and wet-earth marking devices (red, green, and white) for use by FACs in marking targets for strike aircraft. These devices should include the MK-6/63 long-burning ground marker and a long-burning incendiary warhead for the 2.75 inch rocket.[3]

The two major factors which limited effectiveness of aircraft engaged in strike/MIGCAP over North Vietnam were: (1) the presence of an effective integrated enemy air defense system; and (2) the necessity of conducting strikes in visual weather conditions (high ceilings and good visibilities) to insure a CEP on the order of 400-500 feet and acceptable survival probabilities. The success of the strike effort was proportional to the Air Force's ability to cope with the AAA and SAM defenses and to counter the enemy interceptor force. The absence of accurate night and weather bombing capability required that strikes be confined to those days when they could be visually conducted; the tactics imposed by enemy defenses further limited strike opportunities to days when weather was suitable for countering these tactics. [4/]

In view of the rugged terrain in some of the operational areas in SEA, assignment of specific operational areas of responsibility to certain Wings would have been advantageous. The ability of an aircrew to strike/interdict an area with good results, was highly dependent upon their knowledge and familiarity with that area. The success of this concept was proved conclusively during an interdiction program conducted in Route Package I and TALLY HO areas. [5/]

It was the unanimous opinion of all representatives from units involved in out-country, night operations that dedicated night crews should be employed. However, there was a wide divergence of opinion as to the length of time these crews should remain night-dedicated. Suggestions varied from six-to-eight weeks at a time, to that of assigning a squadron a permanent night mission. In the final analysis, because of the wide divergence in missions, the representatives agreed that the final decision should rest with the Wing Commander.[6/]

Every attempt was made to perfect tactics and techniques which would attain the maximum possible navigation capability, electronic protection, and bombing accuracy with the equipment possessed. Results from previous evaluations of this problem have indicated that the basic solution lay in more sophisticated avionics. Therefore, to satisfy future requirements for an effective and reliable all-weather weapons delivery system, the scientific community must design and develop systems capable of solving the navigation, electronic defense, and target acquisition/attack problems.[7/]

The requirement for an all-weather and night strike capability was well established during past wars. Nevertheless, a suitable weapons system had not been procured for that specific purpose; instead, aircrews were required to improvise. An adequate solution to the all-weather ordnance delivery problem should be pursued with vigor.

FOOTNOTES

INTRODUCTION

1. (S) Ltr, Deputy Comdr for Operations, 12th TFW to 7AF (DOA), subj: Information for Air Staff Report, 17 Dec 68.

2. (S) Atch to 7AF (DPLR) Ltr, subj: Quarterly SEAOR Review, 26 Dec 68.

3. (S) Report, Conference Chairman, 7AF (DOT), subj: Minutes of 7AF Night Combat Operations Conference, 9-10 Sep 68.

CHAPTER I

1. (U) Report, Aerospace Studies Institute, Air University, Maxwell AFB, Ala., "Climatology Study of SEA", Aug 68.

2. Ibid, pp 1-2.

3. Ibid, pg 2.

4. Ibid, pg 2.

5. Ibid, pg 3.

6. Ibid, pg 3.

7. Ibid, pg 10.

8. Ibid, pg 10.

9. Ibid, pg 11.

10. Ibid, pg 11.

11. Ibid, pg 11.

12. Ibid, pg 12.

13. Ibid, pp 13-14.

14. Ibid, pg 14.

15. Ibid, pp 14-15.

16. Ibid, pp 15-16.

17.   Ibid, pg 16.

18.   Ibid, pg 16.

19.   Ibid, pg 16.

CHAPTER II

1. (S)   End of Tour Report, Col Paul C. Watson, Commander, 366th Tactical Fighter Wing, Da Nang AB, South Vietnam, 17 Jan 68-2 Jan 69. (Hereafter cited: End of Tour Report, Comdr, 366th TFW.)

2. (S)   Ltr, Dep Comdr for Operations, 31st Tactical Fighter Wing to 7th AF (DOA), subj: Information for Air Staff Report, 17 Dec 68. (Hereafter cited: 31st TFW Ltr.)

3. (S)   Ltr, Deputy Comdr for Operations, 8th Tactical Fighter Wing to 7th AF (DOA), subj: Information for Air Staff Report, 14 Dec 68. (Hereafter cited: 8th TFW Ltr.)

4. (S)   Ltr, Dep Comdr for Operations, 366th Tactical Fighter Wing to 7th AF (DOA), subj: Project CHECO, "The Impact of Night and Weather on Air Operations in SEA", 18 Dec 68. (Hereafter cited: 366th TFW Ltr.)

5. (S)   Ltr, Actg Dep Comdr for Operations, 37th Tactical Fighter Wing to 7AF (DOA), subj: Information for Air Staff Report", The Impact of Weather and Darkness on Air Operations in SEA", 14 Dec 68. (Hereafter cited: 37th TFW Ltr.)

6. (S)   Ltr, Dep Comdr for Operations, 35th Tactical Fighter Wing to 7AF (DOA), subj: Night/Weather Operations, 14 Dec 1968. (Hereafter cited: 35th TFW Ltr.)

7.   Ibid.

8. (S)   Ltr, Dep Comdr for Operations, 355th Tactical Fighter Wing to 7AF (DOA), subj: Inputs for Air Staff Report", The Impact of Weather and Darkness on Air Operations in SEA", 16 Dec 68. (Hereafter cited: 355th TFW Ltr.)

9. (S)   Ltr, Dep Comdr for Operations, 388th Tactical Fighter Wing to 7AF (DOA), subj: The Impact of Weather and Darkness on Air Operations in SEA, 21 Dec 68. (Hereafter cited: 388th TFW Ltr.)

10.   Ibid.

11.   Ibid.

12.   Ibid.

13. (S)   Ltr, Dep Comdr for Operations, 460th Tactical Reconnaissance Wing to 7AF (DOA), subj: Information for Air Staff Report, 15 Dec 68. (Hereafter cited: 460th TRW Ltr.)

14.   Ibid.

15.   Ibid.

16. (S)   Ltr, Dep Comdr for Operations, 432d TRW to 7AF (DOA), subj: The Impact of Night and Weather on Air Operations in SEA, 15 Dec 68. (Hereafter cited: 432d TRW Ltr.)

17. (SNF)   Ltr, Comdr, 21st SOS, 56th SOW to 56th SOW (DCO), subj: Information for Air Staff Report, 11 Dec 68. (Hereafter cited: 21st SOS Ltr.)

18.   Ibid.

19.   Ibid.

20.   Ibid.

21. (S)   Ltr, Operations Officer, 602d SOS, 56th SOW to 56th SOW (DCD), subj: Night/Weather Survey Reply, 13 Dec 68. (Hereafter cited: 602d SOS Ltr.)

22.   Ibid.

23. (S)   Ltr, Comdr, 606th SOS, 56th SOS to 56th SOW (DCO), subj: Information for Air Staff Report, 11 Dec 68. (Hereafter cited: 606th SOS Ltr.)

24.   Ibid.

25.   Ibid.

26. (S)   8th TFW Ltr.

27. (S)   35th TFW Ltr.

28.   Ibid.

29. (S)   Atch, "8th Tactical Bombardment Squadron Survey Report", to Ltr, Dep Comdr for Operations, 35th Tactical Fighter Wing to 7AF (DOA), subj: Night/Weather Operations, 14 Dec 68. (Hereafter cited: 8th TBS Atch.)

30. _Ibid._

31. (S) Ltr, CHECO Representative, 5th SOS, 632d Combat Support Group to 632d CSG (BXI), subj: Information for Air Staff Report, 12 Dec 68. (Hereafter cited: 5th SOS Ltr.)

32. _Ibid._

33. (S) 366th TFW Ltr.

34. (S) 35th TFW Ltr.

35. _Ibid._

36. (S) 37th TFW Ltr.

37. (S) 355th TFW Ltr.

38. _Ibid._

39. _Ibid._

40. _Ibid._

41. (S) 31st TFW Ltr.

42. (S) 8th TFW Ltr.

43. (S) 366th TFW Ltr.

44. (S) 8th TFW Ltr.

45. (S) 460th TRW Ltr.

46. (S) _Ibid._

47. (S) 432d TRW Ltr.

48. Ltr, Comdr, 1st SOS, 56th SOW to 56th SOW (DCO), subj: Infor for Air Staff Rprt, 13 Dec 68. (Hereafter cited: 1st SOS Ltr.)

49. (S) 432d TRW Ltr.

50. (S) 5th SOS Ltr.

CHAPTER III

1. (S)   8th TFW Ltr.
2.   *Ibid.*
3.   *Ibid.*
4. (S)   31st TFW Ltr.
5.   *Ibid.*
6. (S)   35th TFW Ltr.
7.   *Ibid.*
8.   *Ibid.*
10.   *Ibid.*
11.   *Ibid.*
12.   *Ibid.*
13.   *Ibid.*
14.   *Ibid.*
15.   *Ibid.*
16. (S)   37th TFW Ltr.
17.   *Ibid.*
18.   *Ibid.*
19.   *Ibid.*
20.   *Ibid.*
21. (S)   355th TFW Ltr.
22. (S)   366th TFW Ltr.
23.   *Ibid.*
24.   *Ibid.*
25. (S)   388th TFW Ltr.

26.   <u>Ibid</u>.

27. (S)   460th TRW Ltr.

28.   <u>Ibid</u>.

29. (S)   Ltr, Operations Officer, 22d SOS, 56th SOW to 56th SOW (DCO), subj: Information for Air Staff Report, 12 Dec 68. (Hereafter cited: 22d SOS Ltr.)

30.   <u>Ibid</u>.

31. (S)   606th SOS Ltr.

32. (S)   Atch, 609th SOS, "Inputs for Air Staff Report", to Ltr, Dep Comdr for Operations, 56th SOW to 7AF (DOA), subj: Information for Air Staff Report, 13 Dec 68. (Hereafter cited: 609th SOS Atch.)

33. (S)   22d SOS Ltr.

34. (S)   8th TFW Ltr.

35.   <u>Ibid</u>.

36. (S)   31st TFW Ltr.

37.   <u>Ibid</u>.

38. (SNF)   Seventh Air Force Plan, "FY 1971 7AF Improvement Plan", Nov 68, pp C-45-48.

39.   <u>Ibid</u>, pp C-45-48

40.   <u>Ibid</u>, pp C-45-48

41. (S)   355th TFW Ltr.

42.   <u>Ibid</u>.

43. (S)   606th SOS Ltr.

44.   <u>Ibid</u>.

45. (S)   22d SOS Ltr.

46. (S)   366th TFW Ltr.

47.   <u>Ibid</u>.

48. (S)   388th TFW Ltr.

49.   <u>Ibid.</u>

50. (S)   460th TRW Ltr.

51.   <u>Ibid.</u>

52. (SNF) Ltr, Dep Comdr for Operations, 553d RW to 7AF (DOA), subj: Information for Air Staff Report, 15 Dec 1968. (Hereafter cited: 553d RW Ltr.)

53.   <u>Ibid.</u>

54.   <u>Ibid.</u>

55.   <u>Ibid.</u>

56.   <u>Ibid.</u>

CHAPTER IV

1. (S)   8th TFW Ltr.

2.   <u>Ibid.</u>

3.   <u>Ibid.</u>

4. (S)   31st TFW Ltr.

5. (S)   37th TFW Ltr.

6. (S)   31st TFW Ltr.

7.   <u>Ibid.</u>

8. (S)   8th TFW Ltr.

9. (S)   37th TFW Ltr.

10. (S)   8th TFW Ltr.

11. (S)   <u>Ibid.</u>

12. (S)   355th TFW Ltr.

13.   <u>Ibid.</u>

14.   <u>Ibid.</u>

15. (S)　388th TFW Ltr.
16. (S)　8th TFW Ltr.
17. 　　　Ibid.
18. (S)　31st TFW Ltr.
19. 　　　Ibid.
20. (S)　37th TFW Ltr.
21. (S)　366th TFW Ltr.
22. (S)　8th TBS Atch.
23. 　　　Ibid.
24. (S)　432d TRW Ltr.
25. 　　　Ibid.
26. 　　　Ibid.
27. (S)　22d SOS Ltr.
28. (S)　602d SOS Ltr.
29. (S)　609th SOS Atch.
30. 　　　Ibid.
31. (S)　3d TFW Ltr.
32. (S)　31st TFW Ltr.
33. 　　　Ibid.
34. (S)　355th TFW Ltr.
35. (S)　388th TFW Ltr.
36. (S)　Working Paper, 68/10, DOA, 7AF, subj: Pave Way Utility and Cost Effectiveness in SEA, 15 Sep 68. (Hereafter cited: DOA Working Paper Pave Way.)
37. (S)　Special CHECO Rprt, Hq PACAF, DOTEC, "COMBAT SKYSPOT", 9 Aug 67. (Hereafter cited: CHECO Rprt, COMBAT SKYSPOT.)

38. (S) 31st TFW Ltr.
39. (S) 37th TFW Ltr.
40. (S) 3d TFW Ltr.
41. (S) 37th TFW Ltr.
42. (S) 8th TFW Ltr.
43. <u>Ibid.</u>
44. <u>Ibid.</u>
45. (S) 355th TFW Ltr.
46. (S) CHECO Rprt, COMBAT SKYSPOT.
47. <u>Ibid</u>, pg 7.
48. <u>Ibid</u>, pg 12.
49. <u>Ibid</u>, pg 16.
50. (S) Monthly Report, Directorate of Tactical Evaluations, DCS/O, Hq PACAF, "Southeast Asia Air Operations", Nov 68. (Hereafter cited: PACAF Report, Nov 68.)
51. <u>Ibid.</u>
52. (S) 8th TFW Ltr.
53. <u>Ibid.</u>
54. (C) Computer Data, 7AF Directorate of Automated Systems, "Summary of Attack Missions In- and Out-Country, COMBAT SKYSPOT Sorties by Day and Night", 15 Jan 68.
55. (S) 35th TFW Ltr.
56. (S) 8th TBS Atch.
57. (S) 37th TFW Ltr.
58. (S) 31st TFW Ltr.
59. (S) 366th TFW Ltr.

130

CHAPTER V

1. (S) 35th TFW Ltr.
2. Ibid.
3. (S) 355th TFW Ltr.
4. (S) 366th TFW Ltr.
5. (S) 8th TBS Atch.
6. (S) 31st TFW Ltr.
7. (S) 37th TFW Ltr.
8. (S) 366th TFW Ltr.
9. (S) 8th TFW Ltr.
10. (S) End of Tour Report, Comdr 366th TFW.
11. Ibid.
12. Ibid.
13. Ibid.
14. Ibid.
15. (S) 31st TFW Ltr.
16. (S) 35th TFW Ltr.
17. (S) 8th TBS Atch.
18. (S) 355th TFW Ltr.

CHAPTER VI

1. (S) Ltr, Dep Comdr for Operations, 14th SOW to 7AF (DOA), subj: Impact of Night and Weather on Air Operations in SEA, 23 Dec 68. (Hereafter cited: 14th SOW Ltr.)
2. Ibid.
3. Ibid.

4.   Ibid.

5.   Ibid.

6.   Ibid.

7.   Ibid.

8.   Ibid.

CHAPTER VII

1. (C)   Ltr, Director of Operations, 834th Air Division to 7AF (DOA), subj: The Impact of Night and Weather on Air Operations in SEA, 20 Dec 1968. (Hereafter cited: 834th AD Ltr.)

2.   Ibid.

3.   Ibid.

4. (C)   Ltr, Vice Commander, 483d Tactical Airlift Wing to 7AF (DOA), subj: The Impact of Night and Weather on C-7A Airlift Operations in SEA, 14 Dec 1968. (Hereafter cited: 843d TAW Ltr.)

5.   Ibid.

6.   Ibid.

7.   Ibid.

8. (SNF) Ltr, Deputy Commander for Operations, 315th SOW to 7AF (DOA), subj: Information for Air Staff Report, 26 Dec 68. (Hereafter cited: 315th SOW Ltr.)

9.   Ibid.

10.   Ibid.

11.   Ibid.

12.   Ibid.

13.   Ibid.

14. (C)   834th AD Ltr.

15. (SNF) 315th SOW Ltr.

16.   <u>Ibid</u>.

17.   <u>Ibid</u>.

18.   <u>Ibid</u>.

19.   <u>Ibid</u>.

20.   <u>Ibid</u>.

21. (C)   834th AD Ltr.

22.   <u>Ibid</u>.

23.   <u>Ibid</u>.

24.   <u>Ibid</u>.

25.   <u>Ibid</u>.

26.   <u>Ibid</u>.

27.   <u>Ibid</u>.

28. (SNF)   315th SOW Ltr.

CHAPTER VIII

1. (SNF)   Seventh Air Force Plan, "FY 1971 Seventh Air Force Improvement Plan", Nov 1968, pg E-28. (Hereafter cited: 7AF Improvement Plan, FY 71.)

2.   <u>Ibid</u>, pg C-7.

3.   <u>Ibid</u>, pg C-7.

4.   <u>Ibid</u>, pg B-23.

5. (S)   366th TFW Ltr.

6. (S)   Report, Conference Chairman, 7AF (DOT), subj: Minutes of 7AF Night Combat Operations Conference, 9-10 Sep 68.

7.   12th TFW Ltr.

APPENDIX I

(EXTRACTS)

SEVENTH AIR FORCE

NIGHT COMBAT

OPERATIONS CONFERENCE

9 and 10 SEPTEMBER

1968

LT COL NORBERT L. SIMON, DIRECTOR COMBAT TACTICS

CHAIRMAN

OFFICIAL:

    /s/ GORDON F. BLOOD, Maj Gen, USAF
        Deputy Chief of Staff, Operations

    DOWNGRADED AT 3 YEAR INTERVALS
      DECLASSIFIED AFTER 12 YEARS
          DOD DIR. 5200.10

DOT-68-S-181

RECOMMENDED ACTIONS

REFERENCE SECTION III

	ACTION AGENCY
1. When possible, the FAC and Strike pilots should pre-brief together.	DOC
2. Recommend permission for propeller strike aircraft to pursue trucks from Laos into western NVN.	DOC
3. The coding of Delta points should be discontinued. The coding serves no useful purpose and tends to disrupt and confuse the pilots.	DI
4. A-26 Nimrods should be fragged in pairs for mutual support.	DOC

RECOMMENDED ACTIONS

REFERENCE SECTION IV

1. Length of time night crews remain dedicated be left to the discretion of the individual wing commander.	DO
2. Every effort be expended to maintain crew integrity among dedicated night crews (i.e., same A/C and Pilot.)	Wing Commanders
3. The use of navigators at night be restricted to Commando Nail and Combat Sky Spot missions.	Wing Commanders
4. Targets be defined and jet fighters be used against point targets, truck parks and storage areas.	DOC
5. Fleeting targets, such as trucks and WBLC, be the primary targets for slow movers.	DOC
6. That a percentage of the fast movers be committed to an airborne alert to provide a:	DOC

    a. Fast reaction force for priority targets.

    b. Force capable of defending the slow movers against enemy defenses.

7. All night interdiction aircraft should be loaded with soft incendiary type munitions.	DOC
8. Aircraft loaded with hard bombs should be limited to pre-planned point or area type interdiction targets.	DOC

ACTION AGENCY

9. When iron bombs are used they should have fuze extenders attached when possible. DOC

10. Use of flares on the strike aircraft should be discontinued when the flight is fragged with a FAC. DOC

11. When fragging the wings to dispense the CBU-2 munitions, the phase of the moon must be taken into consideration. Moon light is essential for the effective and safe employment of this munition. DOC

12. A firm battle plan should be established and adhered to, and target diverts can thereby be kept to an absolute minimum. DOC

13. Ordnance loads should be standardized. DOC

14. The number of aircraft should be fragged as far in advance as possible. The actual fragging of the target can then be reduced to a realistic six to eight hours. DOC

15. When this program (Commando Hunt) is put into effect, a monthly evaluation meeting should be held at NKP and chaired by 7AF to discuss operational problems and areas for improvement. DOC

RECOMMENDED ACTIONS

REFERENCE SECTION V

1. 7 Air Force should convene a conference to improve the overall air traffic control. The conference should be chaired by 7AF DOCC and representatives should be present from the following agencies:

    a. 505 TACCONGP - GCI/CRP

    b. MSQ - LTD, MILKY, TEEPEE

    c. Marine Air Control Group

    d. SEADRAGON - CTF 77

    e. TFA

    f. Forward Air Controllers

    g. ABCCC

2. A planning group should be convened at NKP to devise a plan for control of

<u>ACTION AGENCY</u>

the increased traffic in the Commando Hunt area. The planning group should be chaired by 7AF and representatives should be present from:

    a. 7AF - DOCC

    b. 7AF- TACT

    c. ABCCC

    d. Forward Air Controllers

    e. GCI

    f. Strike Wings - one representative from each type strike aircraft.

RECOMMENDED ACTIONS

REFERENCE SECTION VI

1. Full utilization of reconnaissance should be used for pre and post-strike BDA. The use of IR should be considered acceptable.   DOC

2. All airborne alert aircraft should be scheduled for air refueling. This will provide best utilization of the alert aircraft.   DOC

3. The method of distribution, routing and schedule of a Scatback for pre-strike, surveillance and BDA intelligence should be reviewed by 7AF with a view toward providing the most recent imagery immediately to the strike wings, direct from the reconnaissance wings.   DI

4. 7AF should consider assigning photo interpreters, appropriately equipped with PI hardware, to each of the strike wings.   DI

5. 7AF should make a special effort to insure that operating units target folders are kept up to date with the addition of current photographs. Numerous complaints have been received from pilots concerning old photographs in target folders.   DI

RECOMMENDED ACTIONS

REFERENCE SECTION VII

1. Use the 366TFW F-4s to work with Marine A-6s since they are collocated at Danang. This would allow aircrews to brief and debrief

                                                                    ACTION AGENCY

together in addition to facilitating rendezvous. Taking off   DOC
together would also allow longer TOTs.

2. Use SPUD to initially acquire targets. SPUD can pass loca-   DO
tion to the A-6 aircrew and the A-6 radar can be used for refine-
ment.

3. Use CBU-29/49 to mark the target. The delayed fuzing would   DO
provide a suitable reference for a long enough time to allow the
F-4s to acquire the target. Flares should not be used. Finned
BLU-27 napalm would be a substitute when ballistics have been
determined for use in the A-6.

4. These missions should be conducted along the coastal plains.   DO
This is the optimum area for the A-6 radar.

<u>NOTE</u>:

Although the minutes of the 7AF 9 and 10 September Night Operations Conference
have been designated official the recommended actions have not as yet been
approved by the DCS/O. It is requested that each action agency review
respective recommended actions and submit to the DCS/O NLT three weeks from
receipt of these minutes final comments and/or final courses of action.

                                        /s/ NORBERT L. SIMON
                                            Lt Col   USAF
                                            Director Combat Tactics

                                ****

NIGHT TACTICS COMMITTEE

1. The committee purpose was to discuss and evaluate the tactics used in the night interdiction program.

2. To arrive at logical conclusions concerning night tactics, and to properly support the Commando Hunt program in the future, the committee felt that some assumptions had to be agreed upon. These were:

   a. Strike aircraft should be permitted to operate against preplanned targets without the use of a FAC.

   b. Commando Nail and Combat Sky Spot missions should be permitted to strike preplanned targets without the use of a FAC.

   c. Aircraft involved in the Commando Hunt program should be permitted to strike targets of opportunity within defined areas and along the major LOCs, without the use of a FAC.

3. The committee decided to discuss the night tactics subjects by breaking them down into four (4) basic areas:

   a. Dedicated night crews

   b. Targets

   c. Ordnance

   d. Tactics

4. Dedicated Night Crews: It was the unanimous opinion of all members of the committee that dedicated night crews should be employed. However there was a wide divergence of opinion as to the length of time these crews should remain night dedicated. It was agreed these night crews must, at times, fly some day missions in order to become familiar with terrain and also maintain their day capability. Suggestions varied concerning length of time crews should remain night dedicated. Dedication periods suggested ranged from six (6) to eight (8) weeks at a time, to that of squadrons being permanently assigned the night mission. It was agreed that because of the wide divergence in missions the actual degree of dedication should be at the discretion of the Wing Commander. It was suggested that navigators be restricted from performing duties in the night strike aircraft and be limited to night Commando Nail and Combat Sky Spot missions.

APPENDIX II
CLASSIFICATION OF AIRFIELDS

TYPE 1-(MINIMUM OPERATIONAL): The lowest standard of construction utilizing the absolute minimum criteria. Operations on this type of airfield will be hazardous, inefficient and limited to good weather and visibility conditions. Takeoff gross weight will be limited depending upon runway surface, weather conditions and type of aircraft used. Acceleration to Takeoff and stop is not possible. Type 1 airfields should be capable of accepting 700 traffic cycles.

TYPE 2-(MARGINAL OPERATIONS): Airfields constructed to provide a greater margin of safety than Type 1, hence greater support and efficiency. Construction of this type of airfield will support a maximum of 4,000 traffic cycles with less than maximum payloads. Difficult crosswinds, poor visibility, or inclement weather may reduce the effectiveness of support.

TYPE 3-(FULLY OPERATIONAL): A facility constructed to insure established standards of safety and provide a greater efficiency of operation and support. Operations on this type of field are practical under most weather conditions and should be capable of withstanding up to 15,000 traffic cycles.

GLOSSARY

AAA	Antiaircraft
ABCCC	Airborne Battlefield Command and Control
ACS	Air Commando Squadron
AGL	Above Ground Level
AID	Agency for International Development
ARDF	Airborne Radio Direction Finding
ARTC	Air Route Traffic Control
CAO	Civil Aviation Organization
CAP	Civil Air Patrol
CARP	Computer Air Release Point
CAS	Close Air Support
CDS	Container Delivery System
CEA	Circular Error Average
CEP	Circular Error Probable
CRC	Combat Reporting Center; Control and Reporting Center
CS	COMMANDO SABRE
DME	Distance Measuring Equipment
DZ	Drop Zone
ECM	Electronic Countermeasure
FAC	Forward Air Controller
FLR	Forward Looking Radar
FM/DF	Frequency Modulation/Direction Finding
FMU	Fuze Munition Unit
FY	Fiscal Year
GCA	Ground Controlled Approach
GCI	Ground Controlled Intercept
HLZ	Helicopter Landing Zone
ICAO	International Civil Aviation Organization
ILS	Instrument Landing System
IMC	Instrument Meteorological Condition
INS	Inertial Navigation System
IP	Initial Point
IR	Infrared
ISC	Infiltration Surveillance Center
Kts	Knots
LZ	Landing Zone

MEA	Minimum En Route Altitude
MER	Multiple Ejector Rack
MM	Millimeter
Navaids	Navigational Aids
NM	Nautical Mile
OAP	Offset Aiming Point
RAPCON	Radar Approach Control
Recon	Reconnaissance
RHAW	Radar Homing and Warning
RP	Route Package
RTU	Replacement Training Unit
RW	Reconnaissance Wing
SAM	Surface-to-Air Missile
SAR	Search and Rescue
SEA	Southeast Asia
SEAOR	Southeast Asia Operational Requirement
SIF	Search Identification Feature
SLAR	Side-Looking Airborne Radar
SOS	Special Operations Squadron
SOW	Special Operations Wing
SVN	South Vietnam
TACAN	Tactical Air Navigation
TAW	Tactical Airlift Wing
TBS	Tactical Bombardment Squadron
TRW	Tactical Reconnaissance Wing
TER	Tank Ejector Rack
TFW	Tactical Fighter Wing
UHF	Ultra High Frequency
US/FWMF	United States/Free World Military Forces
UTM	Universal Transverse Mercator
VMC	Visual Meteorological Condition
WRCS	Weapons Release Computer Set